Low Cholesterol Cookbook

1000 Days of Easy and Tasty Low-Fat Recipes to Take Care of Your Well-Being without Sacrificing Taste | Includes a Heart Healthy 30-Day Meal Plan from Breakfast to Dinner

Allison Lawrence

Table of Contents

Introduction

Modern living is all about convenience and comfort. These features trickle into our lifestyles, especially the food choices we make. Most of us lead hectic lives that leave little to no time to concentrate on our health. Unfortunately, we are paying dearly for all the conveniences and comforts we are used to. Whether it is a poor diet or a sedentary lifestyle, they contribute to several health problems. One such problem that's become a global concern is high cholesterol. This is also a silent killer because it is a precursor to several harmful health conditions that severely affect our overall quality of life. High cholesterol is incredibly problematic, from increased risk of strokes and heart diseases to diabetes and high blood pressure.

There are multiple factors in life beyond our control. However, one thing you always have complete control over is your health. Don't let high cholesterol levels get in the way of living your life to the fullest. The good news is that there is no time like the present to work on fixing this situation. Choosing a cholesterol-lowering heart-healthy lifestyle is needed for anyone wanting to reduce their cholesterol levels. The first step is understanding cholesterol, its health risks, and tips to reduce it. You don't have to look any further to obtain the needed information. This book will act as your guide and help reduce cholesterol levels.

This book will teach you what cholesterol means, the difference between good and bad cholesterol, and the risk factors associated with high cholesterol. You will also learn about healthy lifestyle habits to not just improve your overall health but also regulate cholesterol levels. You don't have to give up on social commitments for health anymore. Instead, by following the suggestions given in this book, you can eat out without compromising your heart's health.

You will also discover plenty of low-cholesterol recipes. The recipes are divided into different categories for your convenience. From breakfast, salads, and smoothie recipes to soups, stews, chicken, fish, seafood, and meat recipes, this book will act as your one-stop guide to regulating cholesterol levels. You will also learn how to cook without fats and include some healthy desserts into your diet. Apart from this, you will be introduced to a 30-day sample meal plan to make things easier. Once you start cooking with the recipes given in this book, you'll realize that a low cholesterol diet doesn't mean giving up on flavor or taste for the sake of nutrition. Instead, it's simply about making healthy unconscious changes to how and what you cook.

So, are you eager to learn more about reducing your cholesterol levels? If yes, let's get started immediately!

Chapter 1: Understanding Cholesterol

Chances are that you've heard the word cholesterol before or even used it in a regular conversation but do you know what it means?

Cholesterol is a wax-like fatty substance found in all the cells within your body. A little cholesterol is needed to synthesize essential hormones, absorb vitamin D, and produce other substances the body requires for digestion. The human body is self-sufficient, and the cholesterol it needs to take care of its functions is created within. You also obtain it from dietary sources. Eating too much of certain types of fatty foods increases cholesterol levels.

38% of adults in the US have high cholesterol levels, per a report presented by the American Heart Association (Heart Disease and Stroke Statistics, 2022). High cholesterol is not only problematic but the problem is further worsened because it doesn't present itself as any noticeable symptoms. In a way, it is a silent killer. The only means to understand whether your cholesterol levels are balanced or not is to undergo a blood test. You will learn more about this in the later parts of this chapter.

Difference Between Good and Bad Cholesterol

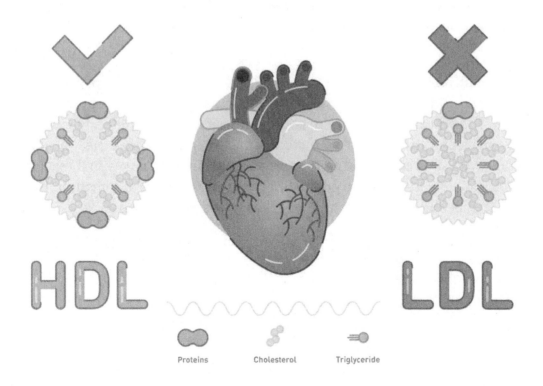

Well, now that you understand what cholesterol means, you might have also come across good and bad cholesterol along with high or low cholesterol. However, not understanding what these terms mean can be detrimental to understanding what you can do to tackle high cholesterol. So, let's understand these differences. Cholesterol is of two types: low-density lipoprotein (LDL) and high-density lipoprotein (HDL).

LDL refers to the fat deposits in the arteries and is commonly dubbed bad cholesterol. The simplest way to distinguish which lipoprotein is good or bad is to associate the "L" in LDL with "lousy." LDL is the bad cholesterol that results in plaque buildup in the blood vessels. This results in their hardening. The arteries also become narrow because of it. When the LDL levels are high, it reduces the flow of blood and oxygen to the heart but results in blockages as well, which results in a condition known as atherosclerosis. Atherosclerosis increases the risk of blood clots in the arteries, which increases the risk of stroke, heart attacks, and chest pain. Also, plaque buildup in arteries reduces the flow of oxygen and blood to all other major organs, not just the heart.

Now, let us get to HDL. HDL is also known as good cholesterol. It becomes easy to remember if you remind yourself that the "H" in HDL stands for "happy." This is not a scientific method but a simple means to better understand the types of cholesterol. This cholesterol is essential to remove the harmful LDL from the body. Think of it as a vacuum cleaner that removes all traces of unnecessary cholesterol. So, if the HDL levels are low or LDL levels are too high, it is harmful to your health.

As mentioned previously, the only means to determine your cholesterol levels is by undergoing a blood test. So, what are the ideal levels of LDL and HDL? The HDL level must be at 60 mg/dl or more. If these levels are below 40 mg/dl, it increases the risk of cardiovascular disorders. Since LDL is bad cholesterol, the lower this number, the better your health. If you don't have any known heart conditions or diabetes, then the LDL shouldn't be higher than 130 mg/dl. If you have any of the conditions mentioned above, including blood vessel disease, then the LDL should never exceed 100 mg/dl.

Causes and Risk Factors

When it comes to high cholesterol levels, different factors are at play. Usually, an unhealthy lifestyle contributes to high cholesterol levels, and the common causes are as follows.

- A poor diet is devoid of essential nutrients but contains plenty of bad fats. One specific type of saturated fat is commonly found in red meat, baked goodies, high-fat dairy products, chocolates, processed foods, and deep-fried foods. Saturated fat is not healthy. Similarly, trans fat is another fat that must be avoided at all costs, and it is found in most processed and fried foods. Consuming too much of such dietary fats increases LDL levels.

- Most of us are guilty of leading a predominantly sedentary lifestyle. A sedentary lifestyle is characterized by little to no physical activity and lots of sitting. This reduces the levels of HDL.

If the HDL levels reduce, your body cannot effectively remove the unnecessary LDL from the blood.

- Another common cause of low HDL is smoking, especially in women. Smoking regularly increases the levels of LDL as well.

Apart from these common causes, some factors also increase the risk of developing high cholesterol.

- Age: Cholesterol levels increase as you age. Even though it is not common, children and teenagers can sometimes develop high cholesterol levels.

- Genetics: High cholesterol is a condition that can run in families. For instance, familial hypercholesterolemia is a genetically passed-on form of cholesterol.

- Body weight: Being obese or overweight drastically increases the levels of undesirable cholesterol.

Now that you are aware of the causes and risk factors, you must understand that high cholesterol does not come with any noticeable symptoms. This is the reason why it is known as a silent killer. The only means to diagnose it is through blood tests. If any of the causes mentioned above or risk factors ring true for you, it's better to regularly check cholesterol levels. This is the only means to take corrective action. As mentioned, high cholesterol results in atherosclerosis. When left unregulated, it can cause several life-threatening health complications such as high blood pressure, stroke, chronic kidney disease, chest pain, heart attack, and peripheral vascular disease.

As scary as high cholesterol sounds, lowering your cholesterol levels is perfectly doable. Read on to learn more!

Foods to Eat and Avoid

The role played by diet cannot be overlooked when it comes to improving your health. If you think of the human body as a vehicle, the food you consume is the fuel that keeps it going. It cannot work as intended if you provide it with the wrong fuel. As mentioned, your body not only synthesizes cholesterol but it's also obtained from different dietary sources. So, some foods are helpful while others are not. In this section, you learn about the foods to eat and avoid managing your cholesterol levels.

What Not to Eat?

Here are all the types of foods you must avoid to lower your cholesterol levels.

Full-Fat Dairy Products

Dairy products are a source of protein, but their fat content cannot be overlooked. Avoid choosing full-fat dairy products such as whole milk, butter, and full-fat yogurt to increase cholesterol levels. Instead, it is better to opt for skimmed and non-fat dairy products.

Red Meat

The cholesterol and saturated fats in red meat such as beef, lamb, and pork are quite high. Regular consumption of red meat is associated with high cholesterol levels.

Fried Foods

Whether it is French fries or fried chicken and chips, ensure that you avoid fried foods to regulate your cholesterol levels. Any food item cooked in a deep fryer in a vat of fat or oil directly increases the consumption of saturated fats and cholesterol.

Processed Meats

Limiting the intake of processed foods in any form is good for your health; this is especially true for processed meats. Processed and deli meats such as sausages, bacon, ham, salami, or hot dogs are made from fatty cuts of meat rich in saturated fats. The added sodium in it for taste further poses a health problem. Cutting them out of your diet and replacing them with wholesome animal foods is better.

Sugary Treats

If you are used to eating sugary foods regularly, you need to avoid doing this. Baked goods and sweets contain high levels of unhelpful saturated fats and cholesterol, whether it is doughnuts, cakes, or cookies. The high sugar in them increases the levels of triglycerides too. Triglycerides are unhealthy body fat associated with an increased risk of cardiovascular disorders.

Alcohol

Alcohol is filled with empty calories and can contribute to weight gain. It is also a known depressant and is detrimental to your mental and physical health. Being overweight or obese increases cholesterol levels. Avoid alcohol or limit it to a single glass of wine or an occasional beer to regulate cholesterol levels.

After going through this list, one thing becomes abundantly clear: the need to stay away from all processed and prepackaged foods. They are not only devoid of essential nutrients but contain additives and harmful fats. Also, avoiding the foods given in this section will improve your overall health and not just lower your cholesterol levels.

What to Eat?

Now that you know all the foods to avoid, let's look at the foods you can eat.

Whole Grains

If you want to reduce the risk of cardiovascular disorders and cholesterol levels, increase the consumption of whole grains. Instead of their processed variants, including flour and products made with it, replace them with whole grains. A specific type of healthy soluble fiber known as beta-glucan is present in whole grains such as barley and oats. Beta-glucan reduces the levels of LDL.

Fruits and Vegetables

Adding a variety of fruits and vegetables to your daily diet is one of the best dietary changes you can make. They are not only filled with essential nutrients and vitamins but contain helpful antioxidants too. Ensure that your daily diet consists of fruits and vegetables of different colors. The soluble fiber in them helps reduce cholesterol absorption and tackle LDL levels.

Healthy Fats

Fats usually get a bad rap, but all fats aren't the same. In the previous section, you were introduced to a list of foods rich in unhealthy saturated fats. Some foods contain heart-healthy omega-3 fatty acids and other mono and poly-unsaturated fats that increase HDL levels. This, in turn, makes it easier for your body to manage LDL levels. Some healthy fats that must be a part of your daily diet are avocados, nuts and seeds, olives, and vegetable oils. Apart from this, increase the consumption of naturally fatty fish and seafood such as mackerel, sardines, trout, salmon, and shrimp. Use the above-mentioned healthy fats for cooking as well.

Beans and Legumes

Beans and legumes such as chickpeas, lentils, pinto beans, black beans, navy beans, and so on are incredible sources of protein and soluble fiber. Regular consumption of these ingredients is known to reduce cholesterol levels and improve the functioning of the digestive system. Also, they can be easily incorporated into different dishes ranging from soups and stews to casseroles and dips!

Nuts

Regularly eating nuts such as almonds, walnuts, hazelnuts, pecans, pistachios, and pine nuts is good for your health. The healthy fats in them don't increase the levels of harmful LDL. However, moderation is key when it comes to eating nuts and even seeds, for that matter.

Lean Meat

Instead of red meat, swap it with lean meat such as lean poultry, such as skinless chicken and turkey. You can have non-fatty cuts of red meat but in limited portions. Instead of meat, it would be better to shift to shellfish and seafood to obtain the needed protein and healthy fats.

When it comes to lowering cholesterol levels, understand that there is no one specific category of foods that will help. Instead, you need to focus on a well-rounded and wholesome diet along with the quality of ingredients you eat.

Better Eating and Lifestyle Habits

Here are some simple habits you can develop to lower cholesterol levels and improve your overall health and well-being!

- Start by reducing saturated fats and eliminating trans-fats while increasing the consumption of heart-healthy omega-3 fatty acids. By consuming more wholesome and unprocessed foods, you can rest easy knowing that your body is getting its essential nutrients. Ensure that your daily diet consists of all the different categories of foods you were introduced to in the previous chapter.

- Start exercising regularly. Even if it is for only 20–30 minutes per day, do it. Regular exercise gets your body moving and increases HDL levels. Whether it is brisk walking, jogging, swimming, running, dancing, or even playing a sport, go ahead and do it. Regular physical activity is associated with better mental health and cognitive functioning too.

- If you are used to smoking or have been wanting to quit but never got around to it, there is no time like the present to make this change! Kicking this extremely bad habit is essential for your overall health. Also, once you quit smoking, your blood pressure levels will be stable, and the risk of cardiovascular disorders also reduces.

- Maintain your ideal body weight. If you are overweight or obese, focus on weight loss to reduce cholesterol levels. By exercising regularly and eating a well-balanced diet, achieving weight loss and its maintenance also becomes easy.

Tips for Dining Out

Are you worried about giving up on your social life and commitments to health? Well, you don't have to be! You can manage your cholesterol levels even when you eat out, provided you don't mind making a few conscious changes. Use these tips to ensure that your cholesterol levels don't increase while eating out.

- Carefully go through the menu and look for low-fat or healthy foods with ingredients you were introduced to in the previous section.

- Avoid those food items if you notice the terms crispy, pan-fried, escalloped, or buttery. Instead, opt for items with the terms grilled, steamed, boiled, stir-fried, poached, grilled, baked, or roasted.

- Don't hesitate to talk to the server about the foods you must avoid when in doubt. Also, pay attention to the portion sizes. You needn't eat everything served on the plate if you are full.

- Any food items, sauces, dips, or dressings rich in sodium or salt must be avoided. Whether it is fish or soya sauce, avoid high-sodium condiments. Instead, it is always better to ask for the gravy, sauce, or dressing on the side instead of it being directly served on the dish.

- Eating a salad is healthy, right? Well, the dressing with the salad matters a lot! Balsamic vinegar or any vinaigrette dressing is healthy when compared to creamy ones such as Caesar dressing. Avoid creamier dressings; always ask for it on the side if unavoidable.

- Also, skip the breadbasket or other bread-based dishes on the menu, especially if made with processed flour.

Chapter 2: Breakfast Recipes

Start your day on the right note by using the low-cholesterol and delicious breakfast recipes given in this chapter!

<u>Loaded Quinoa Breakfast Bowl</u>

Serves: 2

Nutritional values per serving: 1 bowl
Calories: 475, Fat: 13 g, Cholesterol: 0 mg, Carbohydrates: 83 g, Fiber: 10 g, Protein: 13 g

Ingredients:
- ½ cup quinoa, rinsed
- 1 ½ cups water, divided
- ¼ cup dried goji berries or cranberries
- ½ cup unsweetened almond milk + extra to serve
- ¼ teaspoon ground cinnamon
- ½ cup fresh or frozen unsweetened blueberries
- ⅛ cup slivered almonds
- ⅛ cup chopped walnuts
- ⅛ cup fresh pumpkin seeds
- 2 small bananas
- 2 tablespoons maple syrup
- ¼ teaspoon vanilla extract

Directions:

1. Pour a cup of water into a saucepan. Place the saucepan over medium heat.
2. When water starts boiling, stir in quinoa.
3. Turn down the heat and cook until dry. Turn off the heat. Take a fork and loosen the grains.
4. Place dried berries in a bowl. Pour remaining water over the berries and let the berries rehydrate for 10 minutes.
5. Mash one banana. Cut the other banana into semi-circles.
6. Combine mashed banana, cinnamon, maple syrup, and vanilla in a bowl.
7. Stir in walnuts, blueberries, goji berries, pumpkin seeds, almonds, and banana slices.
8. Divide into two bowls. Pour some extra almond milk on top and serve.

Chocolate Almond Bars

Serves: 6

Nutritional values per serving: 1 bar
Calories: 166, Fat: 6 g, Cholesterol: 1 mg, Carbohydrates: 17.6 g, Fiber: 2.9 g, Protein: 12.8 g

Ingredients:
- 3 ounces almonds
- ½ teaspoon ground cinnamon
- 1 scoop plant based vanilla protein powder - tablespoon
- 1 ounce dairy-free chocolate chips (optional)
- a pinch sea salt
- ⅓ cup rolled oats
- 3 ½ tablespoons maple syrup

Directions:

1. Grease a small square pan (4–5 inches) with cooking spray. Place a sheet of parchment paper inside the pan.
2. Chop 1 ounce almonds and set aside.
3. Add remaining almonds and salt into a blender or food processor and process until sticky.
4. Add cinnamon, protein powder, oats, and maple syrup and continue blending until well incorporated.
5. Spread the mixture evenly in the prepared pan. Scatter chopped almonds on top of the mixture. Press the almonds lightly to adhere.
6. Melt chocolate chips in the microwave and drizzle over the mixture.
7. Chill for 30–40 minutes. Cut into four to five bars and serve.
8. Store leftovers in an airtight container in the refrigerator.

Overnight Peach Oatmeal

Serves: 3

Nutritional values per serving: ¾ cup
Calories: 163, Fat: 2 g, Cholesterol: 0 mg, Carbohydrates: 31 g, Fiber: 4 g, Protein: 5 g

Ingredients:
- 2 cups water
- ½ cup vanilla soy milk or vanilla almond milk
- ⅛ teaspoon salt
- 1 medium peach, sliced or 1 ½ cups frozen unsweetened sliced
- ½ cup steel-cut oats
- 1 ½ tablespoons brown sugar
- ⅛ teaspoon vanilla extract or almond extract

Directions:

1. Combine water, milk, salt, oats, brown sugar, and vanilla extract in a saucepan. Place the saucepan over medium heat, stirring often until the oats are cooked. Turn off the heat.
2. Add peaches and mix well. Serve in bowls with toppings of your choice if desired.

Breakfast Parfaits

Serves: 2

Nutritional values per serving: 1 glass
Calories: 277, Fat: 4 g, Cholesterol: 3 mg, Carbohydrates: 60 g, Fiber: 6 g, Protein: 5 g

Ingredients:
- 1 cup chopped fresh pineapple chunks
- ½ cup fresh or frozen raspberries
- ½ cup sliced ripe banana
- ½ cup nonfat vanilla yogurt
- ¼ cup chopped dates or raisins
- ⅛ cup sliced almonds

Directions:

1. Make layers of the ingredients in two parfait glasses in any colorful manner you prefer, just before serving.

Banana Oatmeal Pancakes

Serves: 4

Nutritional values per serving: 2 pancakes
Calories: 155, Fat: 4 g, Cholesterol: 0 mg, Carbohydrates: 28 g, Fiber: 4 g, Protein: 7 g

Ingredients:
- 1 cup whole-wheat pancake mix
- ¼ cup old-fashioned oats
- ½ large firm banana, finely chopped
- ⅛ cup finely chopped walnuts

Directions:

1. Follow the directions given on the package of pancake mix and prepare the batter.
2. Add walnuts, oats, and banana and mix well.
3. Place a nonstick pan over medium heat. Spray the pan with cooking spray. Scoop out about ¼ cup of the batter and pour on the pan.
4. Cook until the underside is brown. Turn the pancake over and cook the other side as well. Remove the pancake onto a plate and keep warm.
5. Repeat with the remaining batter. You should have eight pancakes in all.
6. Serve with toppings of your choice.

Bulgur Porridge

Serves: 2

Nutritional values per serving: 1 bowl

Calories: 340, Fat: 6.7 g, Cholesterol: 12 mg, Carbohydrates: 58 g, Fiber: 9 g, Protein: 15 g

Ingredients:
- 2 cups 1% milk
- 3 tablespoons dried cherries
- 1 ounce dried apricots, coarsely chopped
- ½ cup bulgur
- ⅛ teaspoon salt
- 4–5 almonds, sliced

Directions:

1. Add bulgur, milk, salt, and cherries into a saucepan.
2. Cook the mixture over medium heat until thick and tender. Stir often.
3. Serve in bowls garnished with almonds and apricots.

Zucchini Tomato Frittata

Serves: 2

Nutritional values per serving: 2 wedges
Calories: 138, Fat: 4 g, Cholesterol: 6 mg, Carbohydrates: 11 g, Fiber: 3 g, Protein: 15 g

Ingredients:
- 3 tablespoons sun-dried tomatoes (not the oil packed ones)
- ¾ cup egg substitute
- 1 green onion, chopped
- crushed red pepper flakes to taste
- salt to taste
- 1 tablespoon grated Parmesan cheese (optional)
- ½ cup boiling water

- ¼ cup 2% cottage cheese
- ⅛ cup chopped fresh basil or ½ tablespoon dried basil
- ½ cup sliced zucchini
- ½ medium red bell pepper, chopped
- ½ cup broccoli florets
- 1 teaspoon canola oil

Directions:

1. Pour boiling water over the sun-dried tomatoes in a bowl. Let it rehydrate for 5 minutes. Drain off the water.
2. Add tomatoes, egg substitute, onion, cottage cheese, salt, and red pepper flakes into a bowl and whisk well.
3. Place a small ovenproof skillet over medium heat. Add oil. When the oil is hot, add broccoli, zucchini, and bell pepper and mix well. Cook until the vegetables are tender.
4. Turn down the heat to low heat. Spread the vegetables all over the pan. Pour the egg mixture over the vegetables.
5. Cover the pan and let it cook until the edges are set and yet wet in the center. Turn off the heat.
6. Meanwhile, set the oven to broil mode and preheat the oven.
7. Uncover and scatter cheese on top. Shift the pan into an oven. Broil uncovered for a couple of minutes, until the center is set.
8. Chop into wedges and serve.

Tomato and Spinach Egg White Omelet

Serves: 1

Nutritional values per serving:
Calories: 110, Fat: 1.92 g, Cholesterol: 0 mg, Carbohydrates: 8.3 g, Fiber: 1.8 g, Protein: 15.4 g

Ingredients:
- ½ cup egg whites
- ⅛ cup finely chopped spinach
- 1 tablespoon finely chopped tomatoes
- 1 tablespoon thinly sliced green onions
- salt to taste
- 1–2 teaspoons water
- pepper to taste

Directions:

1. Beat whites in a bowl adding water, salt, and pepper.
2. Place a small nonstick pan over medium heat. Spray some cooking spray.
3. Add spinach, tomatoes, and green onion and mix well. Cook for about a minute. Transfer into a bowl.
4. Spray some cooking spray into the pan.
5. Pour the egg white mixture into the pan and cook the omelet until it is set.
6. Place the vegetable mixture on one half of the omelet. Fold the other half of the omelet over the filling.
7. Transfer onto a plate and serve hot.

Egg White Muffins

Serves: 6

Nutritional values per serving: 1 muffin
Calories: 49, Fat: 1 g, Cholesterol: 1 mg, Carbohydrates: 3 g, Fiber: 1 g, Protein: 6 g

Ingredients:
- 1 cup egg whites
- ½ cup chopped bell peppers
- ¼ cup diced cherry tomatoes
- Kosher salt to taste
- ½ cup cooked, crumbled turkey sausage
- ½–1 cup chopped spinach
- ¼ cup chopped onion
- pepper to taste

Directions:

1. Preheat the oven to 350°F. Grease six muffin cups with cooking spray.
2. Place a nonstick pan over medium heat. Add oil. When the oil is hot, add onion and bell pepper and mix well. Cook for a couple of minutes.
3. Add spinach, sausage, and tomatoes and mix well. Divide the mixture among the muffin cups.
4. Whisk egg whites in a bowl, adding salt and pepper. Divide the whites among the muffin cups, up to ¾. Stir lightly.
5. Bake the muffins for about 20–25 minutes or until cooked through inside. The muffins will puff up.
6. Let the muffins cool for a few minutes. Loosen the muffins by running a knife around the edges.
7. Serve with hot sauce and salsa if desired. Store leftovers in an airtight container in the refrigerator. They can last for about 5 days.

Fluffy Egg White Omelet

Serves: 2

Nutritional values per serving: 1 omelet
Calories: 115, Fat: 1.8 g, Cholesterol: 4 mg, Carbohydrates: 7.27 g, Fiber: 1.4 g, Protein: 16.74 g

Ingredients:
- 8 large egg whites
- ¼ teaspoon freshly ground black pepper
- 2 tablespoons grated Parmesan cheese (optional)
- ⅔ cup halved cherry tomatoes
- ½ cup chopped onions
- ¼ cup chopped red and yellow bell peppers
- ¼ teaspoon garlic powder
- ½ teaspoon Kosher salt

Directions:

1. Beat whites in a bowl adding garlic powder, salt, and pepper. Add the vegetables and stir.

2. Place a small nonstick pan over medium heat. Spray some cooking spray.
3. Pour half the egg white mixture into the pan. When the edges are set, turn down the heat to medium-low heat and cook the omelet until it is mostly set but moist in the center.
4. Lift the omelet with a spatula and flip sides. Cook the other side for about a minute. Transfer on to a plate and serve.
5. Cook the other omelet similarly (steps 2–4).

Tofu Scramble

Serves: 2

Nutritional values per serving: ½ recipe
Calories: 233, Fat: 11.8 g, Cholesterol: 0 mg, Carbohydrates: 22.15 g, Fiber: 2 g, Protein: 12.8 g

Ingredients:
- 8–9 ounces extra-firm water packed tofu, drained, dried with paper towels, crumbled
- ½–1 fresh poblano chili pepper, deseeded, chopped
- 1 clove garlic, minced
- ¼ teaspoon ground cumin
- ¼ teaspoon salt or to taste
- ½ cup deseeded, chopped plum tomatoes
- 2 teaspoons olive oil
- 1 small onion, chopped
- ½ teaspoon chili powder
- ¼ teaspoon dried oregano, crushed
- 2 teaspoons lime juice
- chopped fresh cilantro to garnish

Directions:

1. Pour oil into a nonstick skillet and let it heat over medium-high heat. When the oil is hot, add chili pepper, garlic, and onion and stir-fry for a few minutes until the onions are translucent.
2. Stir in chili powder, salt and cumin. Stir constantly for a few seconds until fragrant. Make sure you do not burn the spices.
3. Stir in the tofu. Turn down the heat and let it cook for about 3–4 minutes. Stir occasionally.
4. Add lime juice and tomatoes and stir.
5. Sprinkle cilantro on top and serve.

Chapter 3: Smoothies and Drinks

Smoothies are not only delicious but incredibly nutritious too! Fix yourself a glass of daily nourishment by whipping up a smoothie!

<u>Mixed Berry Smoothie</u>

Serves: 2

Nutritional values per serving: ½ recipe
Calories: 112, Fat: 0.3 g, Cholesterol: 4 mg, Carbohydrates: 19.17 g, Fiber: 1.9 g, Protein: 9.3 g

Ingredients:
- 6 ounces mixed berries (raspberries, strawberries, and blackberries)
- 1 ½ cups skim milk
- 2 tablespoons fat-free Greek yogurt

Directions:

1. Add berries, milk, and yogurt into a blender and blend until you get smooth puree.
2. Pour into glasses and serve with ice.

Cholesterol Crusher Smoothie

Serves: 2

Nutritional values per serving: ½ recipe
Calories: 402, Fat: 15.36 g, Cholesterol: 0 mg, Carbohydrates: 78.8 g, Fiber: 23.1 g, Protein: 16.72 g

Ingredients:
- 1 banana, sliced, frozen
- 4 cups chopped kale
- 2 cups frozen blueberries
- 4 tablespoons cocoa
- 1 cup rolled oats
- a handful almonds
- ¼ cup flaxseeds
- 1 cup water or more if required

Directions:

1. Add kale, blueberries, banana, oats, water, almonds, and cocoa into a blender and blend until you get smooth puree.
2. Pour into glasses and serve with crushed ice if desired.

Avocado Smoothie

Serves: 2

Nutritional values per serving: ½ recipe
Calories: 376, Fat: 24.16 g, Cholesterol: 0 mg, Carbohydrates: 41.2 g, Fiber: 14.1 g, Protein: 6.7 g

Ingredients:
- 1 avocado, peeled, pitted, chopped
- 2 apples, cored, peeled if desired, chopped
- 2 tablespoons plain almond butter
- 1 cup coconut water

Directions:

1. Add avocado, apples, almond butter, and coconut water into a blender and blend until you get smooth puree.
2. Pour into glasses and serve with crushed ice if desired.

Banana Smoothie

Serves: 1

Nutritional values per serving:
Calories: 212, Fat: 3.6 g, Cholesterol: 9 mg, Carbohydrates: 34.2 g, Fiber: 2 g, Protein: 14.2 g

Ingredients:
- ¼ cup 1% low-fat milk
- ½ tablespoon honey
- ½ large banana, sliced, frozen
- ¼ cup crushed ice
- pinch ground nutmeg
- ½ cup fat-free Greek yogurt

Directions:

1. Add milk, honey, banana, ice, and nutmeg into a blender and blend until smooth.
2. Add yogurt and give short pulses until just combined.
3. Pour into a glass and serve.

Pineapple, Mango, and Banana Smoothie

Serves: 2

Nutritional values per serving: ½ recipe
Calories: 556, Fat: 11.41 g, Cholesterol: 0 mg, Carbohydrates: 107.71 g, Fiber: 25.1 g,
Protein: 19.31 g

Ingredients:
- 2 cups freshly brewed green tea, cooled
- 2 cups frozen pineapple chunks
- 1 cup frozen mango chunks
- 4 cups chopped fresh spinach or kale
- 1 ⅓ cups peeled, chopped cucumber
- 1 medium banana, sliced
- ½ teaspoon ground turmeric
- 2 tablespoons chia seeds
- 1 inch fresh ginger, peeled, sliced
- 6 mint leaves
- 2 tablespoons chia seeds
- ice cubes, as required
- 2 scoops plant based protein powder (optional)

Directions:

1. Add green tea, pineapple, mango, spinach, cucumber, banana, turmeric, chia seeds, ginger, mint leaves, ice cubes, and protein powder into a blender and blend until you get smooth puree.
2. Pour into two glasses and serve.

Cucumber and Apple Smoothie

Serves: 1

Nutritional values per serving:
Calories: 105, Fat: 0.45 g, Cholesterol: 0 mg, Carbohydrates: 27.9 g, Fiber: 4.7 g, Protein: 0.93 g

Ingredients:
- 1 apple, peeled, cored, chopped
- 1 cucumber, peeled, sliced
- ½ stalk celery, sliced
- ⅛ cup mint leaves
- 2 tablespoons lemon juice

Directions:

1. Add apple, cucumber, celery, mint, and lemon juice into a blender and blend until you get smooth puree.
2. Pour into a glass and serve.

Papaya, Blueberry, and Avocado Smoothie

Serves: 2

Nutritional values per serving: ½ recipe
Calories: 268, Fat: 18 g, Cholesterol: 0 mg, Carbohydrates: 39.7 g, Fiber: 12.4 g, Protein: 4.21 g

Ingredients:
- 2 cups green tea, cooled
- 1 cup fresh or frozen papaya chunks
- 1 cup fresh or frozen blueberries
- ⅔ avocado, peeled, pitted, chopped
- ½ tablespoon chia seeds
- 1 teaspoon ginger powder
- 1 teaspoon cinnamon powder
- 2 teaspoons honey
- 2 teaspoons turmeric powder or 2 inch piece fresh turmeric, peeled, sliced

Directions:

1. Add green tea, papaya, blueberries, turmeric, avocado, chia seeds, ginger, cinnamon, and honey into a blender and blend until you get smooth puree.
2. Pour in glasses and serve with ice.

Banana and Blueberry Smoothie

Serves: 2

Nutritional values per serving: ½ recipe
Calories: 395, Fat: 15 g, Cholesterol: 17 mg, Carbohydrates: 66.7 g, Fiber: 10.9 g, Protein: 16 g

Ingredients:
- 2 cups oat milk
- 2 teaspoons lecithin granules
- 2 cups blueberries
- ice cubes, as required

- 3 teaspoons LSA (mixture of ground flaxseeds, sunflower seeds, and almond)
- 2 teaspoons psyllium husk
- 1 banana, sliced

Directions:

1. Add oat milk, lecithin granules, blueberries, ice, LSA psyllium husk, and banana into a blender and blend until you get smooth puree.
2. Pour in glasses and serve with ice.

Tropical Green Smoothie

Serves: 2

Nutritional values per serving: ½ recipe
Calories: 478, Fat: 10.6 g, Cholesterol: 0 mg, Carbohydrates: 69.2 g, Fiber: 12.9 g, Protein: 31.7 g

Ingredients:
- 1 banana, sliced, frozen
- 2 cups almond milk
- 2 scoops brown rice protein powder
- 1 cup frozen mango
- 3–4 cups baby spinach leaves
- 1 tablespoon chia seeds

Directions:

1. Add banana, milk, protein powder, mango, spinach, and chia seeds into a blender and blend until you get smooth puree.
2. Pour into glasses and serve with crushed ice.

Chocolate Avocado Smoothie

Serves: 2

Nutritional values per serving: ½ recipe (using nonfat milk)
Calories: 431, Fat: 24.6 g, Cholesterol: 27 mg, Carbohydrates: 38.21 g, Fiber: 11.5 g, Protein: 17.9 g

Ingredients:
- 2 cups soy milk or nonfat milk
- 1 large ripe avocado, peeled, pitted, chopped
- 2 teaspoons hemp seeds or chia seeds
- 1 teaspoon ground cinnamon
- ½ teaspoon cayenne pepper
- 1 cup ice cubes
- 2 tablespoons unsweetened cocoa powder
- 2 scoops chocolate protein powder (unsweetened)
- 1 teaspoon ground nutmeg

Directions:

1. Place avocado, hemp seeds, cinnamon, cayenne pepper, ice cubes, cacao, chocolate protein powder, and nutmeg in a blender.
2. Blend until well combined and smooth.
3. Divide into two glasses and serve.

Cucumber Green Smoothie

Serves: 1

Nutritional values per serving:
Calories: 149, Fat: 11.4 g, Cholesterol: 0 mg, Carbohydrates: 12.4 g, Fiber: 6.7 g, Protein: 3 g

Ingredients:
- ½ cup baby spinach
- ½ inch ginger, peeled, sliced
- juice of ½ lemon
- ½ cup cold water
- ¼ cup chopped cilantro
- 1 small cucumber, peeled, chopped
- ½ cup frozen avocado

Directions:

1. Place spinach, ginger, lemon juice, cold water, cilantro, cucumber, and avocado in a blender.
2. Blend until you get a smooth mixture.
3. Pour into a glass and serve.

Berry Smoothie Bowl

Serves: 1

Nutritional values per serving:
Calories: 155, Fat: 0 g, Cholesterol: 2 mg, Carbohydrates: 35 gFiber: 2 g, Protein: 5 g

Ingredients:
- ½ cup fat-free milk
- ¼ cup frozen unsweetened raspberries
- ½ cup frozen unsweetened strawberries
- sweetener of your choice to taste (optional)
- ice cubes as required

Toppings:
- fresh strawberry slices
- chia seeds or pumpkin seeds
- fresh raspberries
- sliced nuts

Directions:

1. Add milk, raspberries, strawberries, sweetener, and ice cubes into a blender and blend until smooth.
2. Pour into a bowl. Garnish with suggested toppings and serve.

Turmeric Jamu

Serves: 1

Nutritional values per serving:
Calories: 103, Fat: 0.42 g, Cholesterol: 0 mg, Carbohydrates: 26.36 g, Fiber: 2.4 g, Protein: 1.16 g

Ingredients:
- 1 tablespoon turmeric powder
- 2 tablespoons fresh lemon juice
- 1 cup water
- ½ teaspoon ground ginger
- 1 tablespoon honey

Directions:

- Pour water into a pan and let it come to a boil over medium heat.
- When water starts boiling, stir in turmeric and turn down the heat to low heat. Let it simmer for 3 minutes. Stir in ginger.
- Let the mixture simmer until it boils down to ½ cup. Turn off the heat.
- Add honey and lemon juice and stir.
- Pour into a cup and serve. You can serve it hot or warm or chilled.

Lemon, Garlic and Ginger Drink

Serves: 1

Nutritional values per serving:
Calories: 53, Fat: 0.47 g, Cholesterol: 0 mg, Carbohydrates: 13.65 g, Fiber: 1 g, Protein: 1.23 g

Ingredients:
- 2 small lemons
- 2 large cloves garlic, cut into halves
- 1 inch fresh ginger, peeled, grated
- 2 ½ cups spring water
- warm water, as required
- 1 teaspoon baking soda

Directions:

1. Soak lemons in a bowl of warm water and add baking soda to it. Let them soak for at least 15 minutes.
2. Rinse the lemons well in running water. Peel off the skin and chop lemons into pieces. Discard the seeds.
3. Add ginger, garlic, and lemon into a blender and blend until well combined and somewhat smooth.

4. Pour the blended mixture into a pot. Add water and stir. Place the pot over medium heat.
5. When the mixture just comes to a boil, turn off the heat. Place cheesecloth over a strainer. Place the strainer over a bowl. Pour the hot mixture into the strainer and strain.
6. Pour the strained mixture into a jar. When it cools down, fasten the lid and place it in the refrigerator.
7. Drink ½ cup of this mixture 30 minutes before lunch and have it once in the evening. Have it continuously for 3 weeks. Give a break for 8 days. Repeat once again.

Hibiscus Tea

Serves: 1

Nutritional values per serving:
Calories: 3, Fat: 0 g, Cholesterol: 0 mg, Carbohydrates: 0.55 g, Fiber: 0 g, Protein: 0 g

Ingredients:
- 1 ½ teaspoons dried hibiscus flowers or petals of 2 fresh red hibiscus flowers
- 1 cup hot water

Directions:

1. Combine hibiscus and hot water in a cup. Cover the cup and let it infuse for 5 minutes.
2. Strain the tea and serve.

Chapter 4: Snacks and Sides

Snacks don't have to be unhealthy. Using the different recipes in this chapter, you can eat your way to a healthier you!

Oatmeal Energy Bites

Serves: 2–3

Nutritional values per serving: 2 bites per serving
Calories: 278, Fat: 14 g, Cholesterol: 0 mg, Carbohydrates: 30 g, Fiber: 4 g, Protein: 10 g

Ingredients:
- ½ cup rolled oats
- 1 tablespoon honey
- ¼ cup nut butter
- ⅛ cup chopped nuts or dried fruit or seeds (optional)

Directions:

1. Combine oats, honey, nut butter, and optional ingredients if using and mix well.
2. Make 6–8 portions of the mixture and shape into balls.
3. Place on a plate and chill until use.

Guacamole with Sliced Veggies

Serves: 2–3

Nutritional values per serving: ¼ cup guacamole with 1 cup vegetables
Calories: 131, Fat: 8 g, Cholesterol: 0 mg, Carbohydrates: 15 g, Fiber: 9 g, Protein: 3 g

Ingredients:
- 1 ripe avocado, peeled, pitted, mashed
- 1 tablespoon lime juice
- ⅛ cup diced tomatoes
- ⅛ cup diced onion
- 1 clove garlic, minced
- 1 tablespoon chopped fresh cilantro
- 2–3 cups fresh vegetable sticks (like carrot, cucumber, celery, etc. cut into sticks)
- salt to taste

Directions:

1. To make guacamole: Combine avocado, lime juice, tomatoes, garlic, salt, and cilantro in a bowl.
2. Serve guacamole with vegetable sticks.

Roasted Chickpeas

Serves: 2–3

Nutritional values per serving: ½ cup
Calories: 184, Fat: 6 g, Cholesterol: 0 mg, Carbohydrates: 27 g, Fiber: 5 g, Protein: 6 g

Ingredients:
- 1 cup cooked or canned chickpeas, drained
- salt to taste
- spices of your choice to taste (optional)
- 2 teaspoons olive oil

Directions:

1. Preheat the oven to 400°F. Line a baking sheet with parchment paper.
2. Toss chickpeas with oil. Add salt and spices and mix well.
3. Spread the chickpeas on the baking sheet and place it in the oven.
4. Set the timer for 30 minutes or bake until crisp.
5. Cool completely and serve.

Edamame

Serves: 2

Nutritional values per serving: ½ recipe
Calories: 240, Fat: 10 g, Cholesterol: 0 mg, Carbohydrates: 16 g, Fiber: 10 g, Protein: 20 g

Ingredients:
- 2 cups edamame in pods
- coarse salt to taste

Directions:

1. Steam the edamame pods in the steaming equipment you have for about 10–12 minutes or cooked as per your preference.
2. Transfer into a bowl. Sprinkle a bit of salt and toss well.
3. Serve.

Stuffed Mushrooms

Serves: 6–7

Nutritional values per serving: 1 stuffed mushroom
Calories: 60, Fat: 4 g, Cholesterol: 0 mg, Carbohydrates: 8.5 g, Fiber: 0.8 g, Protein: 2.2 g

Ingredients:
- ¼ cup black rice or wild rice or brown rice, rinsed well
- 6–7 baby Portobello or white button mushrooms, cleaned, discard stems
- 2 tablespoons raw walnuts, finely chopped
- 3 teaspoons olive oil + extra to drizzle
- ½ cup vegetable stock
- pepper to taste
- 2 tablespoons grated vegan Parmesan cheese + extra to top
- 1 teaspoon garlic, finely minced
- salt to taste

Directions:

1. Pour vegetable stock in a pan and bring to a boil over medium heat. Add wild rice and stir.
2. Lower heat and cover with a lid. Simmer until the rice is cooked.
3. Preheat the oven to 350°F. Line a baking sheet with parchment paper.
4. Brush the mushrooms with olive oil. Place on the baking sheet, with the stem side on top and put it in the oven.
5. Set the timer for about 10 minutes.
6. To make the filling: Mix together in a bowl, vegan Parmesan cheese, the rice, cheese, walnuts, olive oil, garlic, salt and pepper.
7. Divide and fill this mixture in the mushroom caps.
8. Sprinkle some more Parmesan cheese on top if desired.
9. Bake until the cheese is brown.
10. Serve.

Trail Mix

Serves: 3

Nutritional values per serving: ¼ cup (2 tablespoons nuts with 2 tablespoons dried fruit)
Calories: 137, Fat: 7 g, Cholesterol: 0 mg, Carbohydrates: 19 g, Fiber: 3 g, Protein: 4 g

Ingredients:
- ⅛ cup chopped walnuts
- ⅛ cup chopped almonds
- ⅛ cup pecans
- ⅛ cup pumpkin seeds
- ⅛ cup raisins
- ⅛ cup chopped apricots

Directions:

1. Combine nuts, seeds, and dried fruit in an airtight container. Store at room temperature.

Nutty Apples

Serves: 2

Nutritional values per serving: 1 apple with 1 tablespoon peanut butter
Calories: 210, Fat: 9 g, Cholesterol: 0 mg, Carbohydrates: 34 g, Fiber: 6 g, Protein: 5 g

Ingredients:
- 2 apples, cored, thinly sliced
- 2 tablespoons peanut butter or any other nut butter of your choice

Directions:

1. Melt the peanut butter in a microwave for 15–20 seconds.
2. Place apple slices on a serving platter. Drizzle melted peanut butter over the apples and serve.

Cholesterol Busting Bars

Serves: 4

Nutritional values per serving: 1 bar
Calories: 178.6, Fat: 2.9 g, Cholesterol: 0 mg, Carbohydrates: 47.2 g, Fiber: 3.9 g, Protein: 2.7 g

Ingredients:
- ⅛ teaspoon salt
- ¼ cup honey
- 1 tablespoon whole-wheat flour
- ¼ cup raisins
- ¾ cup oats
- 1 ½ tablespoons non dairy butter, melted

Directions:

1. Preheat the oven to 350°F. Place a sheet of parchment paper on a small baking sheet or loaf pan.
2. Combine salt, honey, wheat flour, raisins, oats, and non dairy butter in a bowl.
3. Spread the mixture on the baking sheet. Place the baking sheet in the oven and set the timer for 25 minutes.
4. Cut into four equal bars and serve.

Easy Rolls

Serves: 3

Nutritional values per serving: 1 roll
Calories: 111, Fat: 4 g, Cholesterol: 3 mg, Carbohydrates: 16 g, Fiber: 0 g, Protein: 3 g

Ingredients:
- ½ cup self-rising flour
- 1 tablespoon mayonnaise
- ¼ cup 2% milk
- ¼ teaspoon sugar

Directions:
1. Preheat the oven to 450°F. Grease three muffin cups with some cooking spray.
2. Combine flour, mayonnaise, milk, and sugar in a bowl.
3. Divide the batter among the muffin cups.
4. Place the muffin cups in the oven and set the timer for 12–14 minutes or until cooked through. To check if it is cooked through, insert a toothpick in the center of the roll and remove it. Check if there are any particles stuck on it. If you find any particles stuck on it, you need to bake for a couple of minutes longer else turn off the oven and take out the muffin cups.
5. Cool for a few minutes. Remove the rolls from the muffin cups and serve.

Peanut Rice

Serves: 2

Nutritional values per serving: ½ recipe
Calories: 283, Fat: 10.5 g, Cholesterol: 0 mg, Carbohydrates: 40 g, Fiber: 4 g, Protein: 9 g

Ingredients:
- ½ cup uncooked basmati rice
- ¼ teaspoon salt
- ¼ cup frozen peas, thawed
- 1 ⅛ cups water
- ⅛ teaspoon turmeric powder
- ¼ cup roasted peanuts

Directions:

1. Cook rice in a pot adding salt, water, and turmeric over medium heat. Cook covered until tender.
2. Add peas during the last 2 minutes of cooking. Turn off the heat.
3. Add roasted peanuts and mix well. Serve hot.

Glazed Ranch Carrots

Serves: 5–6

Nutritional values per serving: ¾ cup
Calories: 156, Fat: 8 g, Cholesterol: 20 mg, Carbohydrates: 22 g, Fiber: 1 g, Protein: 1 g

Ingredients:
- 1 pound fresh baby carrots, trimmed
- ¼ cup packed brown sugar
- minced fresh parsley to garnish
- ¼ cup olive oil
- 1 envelope ranch salad dressing mix

Directions:

1. Pour 1 inch of water into a saucepan. Add carrots. Place the saucepan over high heat.
2. When water starts boiling, turn down the heat and cook covered until the carrots are crisp as well as tender. Drain in a colander.
3. Add oil, salad dressing mix, and brown sugar into the saucepan and stir until well combined.
4. Stir in the carrots and place it over medium heat. Cook until the carrots are coated with the glaze.
5. Garnish with parsley and serve.

Orzo with Parmesan and Basil

Serves: 2

Nutritional values per serving: ½ cup
Calories: 285, Fat: 10 g, Cholesterol: 26 mg, Carbohydrates: 38 g, Fiber: 1 g, Protein: 11 g

Ingredients:
- ½ cup uncooked orzo pasta or pearl couscous
- ½ can (from a 14.5 ounces can) chicken broth (use homemade if desired)
- 1 teaspoon dried basil
- thinly sliced fresh basil to garnish
- 1 tablespoon olive oil
- ¼ cup grated low-fat Parmesan cheese
- pepper to taste
- salt to taste

Directions:

1. Pour oil into a heavy skillet and let it heat over medium heat. Add orzo and stir.
2. Cook for a few minutes until light brown, stirring every 2 minutes.
3. Pour broth and stir. When it starts boiling, turn down the heat and cook covered until dry.
4. Add cheese, pepper, salt, cheese, and dried basil and mix well.
5. Garnish with fresh basil and serve.

Roasted Vegetable Medley

Serves: 3

Nutritional values per serving: ⅓ recipe
Calories: 191, Fat: 5 g, Cholesterol: 0 mg, Carbohydrates: 34.6 g, Fiber: 8 g, Protein: 4 g

Ingredients:
- 1 tablespoon olive oil, divided
- ½ large parsnip, peeled, cut into 1 inch pieces
- ½ zucchini, cut into 1 inch slices
- ¼ cup roasted red peppers, cut into 1 inch pieces
- 1 clove garlic, minced
- ¼ teaspoon pepper or to taste
- ½ large yam, peeled, cut into 1 inch pieces
- ½ cup baby carrots
- ½ bunch fresh asparagus, trimmed, cut into 1 inch pieces
- ⅛ cup chopped fresh basil
- ¼ teaspoon Kosher salt

Directions:

1. Preheat the oven to 425°F.
2. Take ½ tablespoon of the oil and brush it on a baking sheet.
3. Scatter parsnip, carrots, and yam on a baking sheet. Place the baking sheet in the oven and set the timer for 30 minutes.
4. Now place asparagus and zucchini on the baking sheet. Pour remaining oil over the zucchini and asparagus and bake for another 20–30 minutes or until the vegetables are tender.
5. Transfer the vegetables into a bowl. Add basil, salt, pepper, and roasted red peppers and toss well.
6. You can serve it hot or warm or at room temperature.

Garlic Herb Cauliflower Rice

Serves: 4

Nutritional values per serving: ¼ recipe
Calories: 26, Fat: 1.7 g, Cholesterol: 0 mg, Carbohydrates: 2.35 g, Fiber: 0.9 g, Protein: 0.9 g

Ingredients:
- ½ medium head cauliflower, grated to rice like texture

- 1 tablespoon extra-virgin olive oil
- ⅛ teaspoon fine sea salt
- ⅓ cup chopped fresh mixed herbs of your choice
- ¼ cup sliced almonds, lightly toasted
- 1 clove garlic, minced
- ¼ teaspoon freshly ground black pepper or to taste
- ½ tablespoon lemon juice or to taste

Directions:

1. Pour oil into a skillet and let it heat over medium heat. When the oil is hot, add garlic and stir constantly for a few seconds until you get a nice aroma.
2. Stir in cauliflower rice, pepper, and salt. Cook until cauliflower rice is crisp as well as tender. Remove from heat.
3. Add herbs, almonds, and lemon juice. Mix well.
4. Serve hot.

Chapter 5: Grains and Legumes

Increasing the consumption of grains and legumes reduces cholesterol levels and improves overall health.

<u>Maple Baked Beans</u>

Serves: 4–5

Nutritional values per serving: ½ cup
Calories: 168, Fat: 3 g, Cholesterol: 6 mg, Carbohydrates: 34 g, Fiber: 5 g, Protein: 4 g

Ingredients:
- ½ medium onion, chopped
- 1 ½ cans (28 ounces each) baked beans
- ½ teaspoon garlic salt
- ½ tablespoon canola oil
- ¾ teaspoon ground mustard
- 6–8 tablespoons maple syrup

Directions:

1. Pour oil into a heavy pan and let it heat over medium heat. When the oil is hot, add onion and cook until translucent.
2. Stir in mustard, beans, and garlic salt. Simmer for about 5 minutes. Stir every now and then.
3. Stir in maple and let it heat for a couple of minutes.
4. Serve hot or warm.

Spanish Rice and Beans

Serves: 3

Nutritional values per serving: ⅓ recipe
Calories: 359, Fat: 7.2 g, Cholesterol: 0 mg, Carbohydrates: 62.6 g, Fiber: 6.5 g, Protein: 11.4 g

Ingredients:
- 1 tablespoon olive oil
- ¼ cup chopped onion
- 1 ½ cups vegetable broth
- ½ can (from a 15 ounces can) kidney beans or black beans, drained, rinsed
- 1 cup dry long grain brown rice
- 1 clove garlic, minced
- ¾ cup tomato based salsa
- ½ teaspoon smoked paprika
- salt to taste
- chopped cilantro to garnish

Directions:

1. Pour oil into a pot and let it heat over medium heat.
2. When the oil is hot, add onion and cook until it turns translucent.
3. Stir in rice, salsa, broth, paprika, and cumin. When it starts boiling, turn down the heat to low heat and cook covered until the rice is tender.
4. Add beans and salt and mix well. Turn off the heat and keep the pot covered for about 10 minutes.
5. Fluff the grains with a fork.
6. Garnish with cilantro and serve.

Kidney Bean Curry

Serves: 4

Nutritional values per serving: ¼ cup curry without serving options
Calories: 418, Fat: 29 g, Cholesterol: 0 mg, Carbohydrates: 34.4 g, Fiber: 12.1 g, Protein: 10.6 g

Ingredients:
- 3 tablespoons olive oil
- 4 cloves garlic, minced
- 1 teaspoon garam masala or curry powder

- ½ cup nondairy milk of your choice
- 2 teaspoon soy sauce
- 2 onions, diced
- 2 inches fresh ginger, grated
- 2 cans (15 ounces each) crushed tomatoes
- 2 cans (15 ounces each) kidney beans, drained
- ½ teaspoon salt or to taste
- crushed red pepper to taste
- cooked grains of your choice to serve (brown rice, quinoa, etc.)

Directions:

1. Pour oil into a pot and let it heat over medium-high heat. When the oil is hot, add onion and cook until soft.
2. Stir in garlic and ginger and cook for a couple of minutes.
3. Stir in garam masala and cook for about 10–15 seconds. Stir in tomatoes, milk, soy sauce, and beans.
4. When the mixture starts boiling, turn down the heat to low heat and cook covered for about 10 minutes. Add salt and crushed red pepper to taste.
5. Garnish with cilantro and serve over hot cooked grains.

Black Bean Corn and Rice Skillet

Serves: 2–3

Nutritional values per serving: ½ recipe
Calories: 354, Fat: 14 g, Cholesterol: 26 mg, Carbohydrates: 45 g, Fiber: 9 g, Protein: 13 g

Ingredients:
- 1 cup cooked or canned black beans, drained, rinsed
- ½ large red bell pepper, finely chopped
- 1 cup frozen corn, thawed
- juice of ½ lime
- ½ tablespoon paprika
- ¼ teaspoon salt or to taste
- ½ tablespoon olive oil
- ¼ cup light sour cream (optional)
- ⅛ cup finely chopped parsley
- 1 clove garlic, minced
- 1 medium red onion, finely chopped
- 1 cup cooked brown rice
- ½ tablespoon chili powder
- ½ tablespoon ground cumin
- ⅛ teaspoon pepper or to taste
- diced avocado to serve (optional)

Directions:

1. Pour oil into a skillet and let it heat over medium-high heat. When the oil is hot, add onion and bell pepper and cook until slightly tender.
2. Stir in garlic and cook for a couple of minutes.

3. Stir in the spices. Keep stirring for about 15 seconds making sure not to burn the spices.
4. Stir in corn, black beans, and rice. Turn down the heat to medium-low heat and heat the rice mixture thoroughly, stirring occasionally.
5. Add lime juice and stir. Garnish with sour cream and avocado if using and serve.

Chickpea Shakshuka

Serves: 3

Nutritional values per serving: ⅓ recipe
Calories: 179, Fat: 3.7 g, Cholesterol: 1 mg, Carbohydrates: 32.63 g, Fiber: 8 g, Protein: 7.7 g

Ingredients:
- ½ tablespoon olive oil or avocado oil
- ¼ red bell pepper, chopped
- ½ can (from a 28 ounces can) tomato puree or diced tomatoes
- ½ tablespoon coconut sugar or maple syrup or Stevia to taste
- 1 teaspoon smoked or sweet paprika
- 1 teaspoon chili powder
- ⅛ teaspoon cayenne pepper (optional)
- ¾ can (from a 15 ounces can) chickpeas, rinsed, drained
- ¼ cup chopped onion or shallots
- 2 cloves garlic, peeled, minced
- 1 ½ tablespoons tomato paste
- salt to taste
- ½ teaspoon ground cumin
- ⅛ teaspoon ground cinnamon
- ⅛ teaspoon ground coriander
- ⅛ teaspoon ground cardamom
- 2–3 kalamata olives or green olives, pitted, halved (optional)

To serve: Optional
- hot cooked brown rice or quinoa or whole-wheat pasta or gluten-free pasta or cauliflower rice
- lemon wedges
- chopped cilantro or parsley

Directions:

1. Pour oil into a skillet and let it heat over medium heat. Add onion, garlic, and bell pepper and cook until slightly tender.
2. Stir in tomatoes, spices, salt, sugar, and tomato paste and mix well. Let it simmer for 2–3 minutes. Stir often.
3. If you are using tomatoes instead of tomato puree, the tomato mixture will be chunky; you can blend about half the mixture with an immersion blender until smooth. If you have no issues about its chunky texture, you need not blend the mixture.
4. Stir in the chickpeas and olives if using. Lower the heat to medium-low and cook for about 15 minutes, stirring often. Turn off the heat.
5. Serve hot with any of the suggested serving options.

Barley and Broccoli Risotto with Lemon and Basil

Serves: 4

Nutritional values per serving: ¼ recipe
Calories: 378, Fat: 14 g, Cholesterol: 0 mg, Carbohydrates: 49 g, Fiber: 7 g, Protein: 11 g

Ingredients:
- 7 ounces pearl barley
- 4 tablespoons canola oil or olive oil
- 4 cloves garlic, peeled, sliced
- 2 tablespoons fresh lemon juice
- 4 teaspoons low-salt vegetable bouillon powder
- 2 large leeks, chopped
- ½ cup loosely packed basil leaves, torn
- 2 cups broccoli florets

Directions:

1. Soak barley in 2 cups of water overnight. Drain the soaked water but retain the water.
2. Add vegetable bouillon powder into the bowl of drained water to make stock.
3. Pour 2 tablespoons of oil into a nonstick pan and let it heat over medium heat.
4. Add leeks and cook until tender. Transfer half the leeks into a bowl and let the remaining leeks remain in the pan.
5. Add barley and the stock and mix well.
6. Cook covered for about 20 minutes on low heat. Add broccoli and stir.
7. Meanwhile, add 2 tablespoons oil, garlic, basil, lemon juice, and about 2 tablespoons of water into the bowl in which the leeks were retained. Blend this mixture in a blender or with an immersion blender until smooth.
8. Add the blended mixture into the pan and mix well. Turn off the heat. Do not cook for more than a minute after adding the blended mixture.
9. Serve hot in bowls.

Chickpeas Sloppy Joes

Serves: 2

Nutritional values per serving: 1 sandwich
Calories: 560, Fat: 8 g, Cholesterol: 0 mg, Carbohydrates: 61.5 g, Fiber: 13.3 g, Protein: 15.5 g

Ingredients:
- ½ teaspoon olive oil
- 1 clove garlic, peeled, minced
- 1 can (15 ounces) chickpeas, rinsed, drained
- 2 tablespoons tomato paste
- 1 tablespoon Sriracha sauce
- 1 teaspoon dried oregano
- salt to taste
- ½ teaspoon dried thyme

- ½ teaspoon liquid smoke
- pepper to taste
- 1 small red onion, diced
- ¼ red bell pepper, diced
- ½ can (from 15 ounces can) fire roasted tomatoes
- 1 tablespoon liquid aminos
- ½ tablespoon maple syrup
- ¾ teaspoon ground cumin
- ½ teaspoon smoked paprika
- ½ tablespoon nutritional yeast (optional)
- 2 whole-wheat hamburger buns, split

Directions:

1. Add chickpeas into a bowl and mash with a fork until slightly chunky. Do not mash until smooth, it should be chunky.
2. Pour oil into a skillet and let it heat over medium heat. When the oil is hot, add onion and garlic and cook until onions are soft.
3. Stir in the chickpeas and bell peppers and cook for a couple of minutes.
4. Stir in tomato paste, Sriracha sauce, oregano, salt, thyme, liquid smoke, pepper, tomatoes, liquid aminos, maple syrup, cumin, paprika, and nutritional yeast if using and let it simmer until thick. Stir occasionally. Turn off the heat.
5. Toast the buns to the desired doneness. Divide the chickpea mixture equally and place on the bottom half of the buns.
6. Cover with the top halves of the buns and serve.

Barley, Beans, and Mushrooms with Beans

Serves: 3

Nutritional values per serving: ⅓ recipe
Calories: 202, Fat: 9.1 g, Cholesterol: 0 mg, Carbohydrates: 39 g, Fiber: 9 g, Protein: 9 g

Ingredients:
- ½ teaspoon olive oil
- ½ cup chopped onion
- 1 clove garlic, minced
- 1 ½ cups vegetable broth
- 1 ½ cups sliced fresh mushrooms
- ¼ cup chopped celery
- ¼ cup uncooked barley
- ½ can (from 15.5 ounces can) white beans, drained
- salt to taste
- pepper to taste

Directions:

1. Pour oil into a pan and let it heat over medium heat.
2. When the oil is hot, add onion, garlic, and celery and cook for a couple of minutes.

3. Stir in the mushrooms. Cook until tender.
4. Add broth and barley and stir. When the mixture starts boiling, turn down the heat to low heat and cook covered until the barley is soft.
5. Add white beans, salt, and pepper and stir. Heat thoroughly.
6. Serve hot.

Black Bean Chili

Serves: 8

Nutritional values per serving: ⅛ recipe
Calories: 344, Fat: 8 g, Cholesterol: 8 mg, Carbohydrates: 54 g, Fiber: 15 g, Protein: 16 g

Ingredients:
- 2 tablespoons olive oil or grapeseed oil
- 2 large red bell pepper, deseeded, chopped
- 2 large yellow bell peppers, deseeded, chopped
- 2 large red onions, chopped
- 2 jalapeño peppers, deseeded, finely chopped
- 4 tablespoons finely ground cornmeal
- 3 teaspoons ground cumin
- ½ teaspoon cayenne pepper or to taste
- 4 teaspoons chili powder or to taste
- 2 teaspoons onion powder
- 4 cloves garlic, peeled, minced
- 2–3 cups vegetable broth
- 4 tablespoons lime juice
- lime wedges to serve
- ½ cup sour cream (or vegan sour cream or cashew cream if you want vegan)
- 4 cans (15 ounces each) black beans with its liquid
- ⅛ cup chopped cilantro + extra to garnish
- salt to taste

Directions:

1. Pour oil into a large pot and let it heat over medium heat. When oil is hot, add onion and cook for a couple of minutes.
2. Stir in jalapeño, bell peppers, and garlic and cook until the edges of the vegetables are slightly charred. It should take around 7–8 minutes. Stir occasionally during this time.
3. Stir in chili powder, cornmeal, cumin, cayenne pepper, and onion powder. Once the spices and cornmeal are well combined, add black beans along with the liquid from the can. Also add the broth and stir well.
4. When the mixture starts boiling, bring down the heat to medium-low and cook covered for about 15 minutes.
5. Add cilantro, salt, and lime juice and stir. Turn off the heat. Let it sit covered for about 5 minutes.
6. Serve in bowls. Garnish with sour cream, cilantro leaves and lime wedge.

Chapter 6: Soups and Stews

Soups and stews are easy to make and make for a comforting and satiating meal too!

<u>Tomato Soup with Beans and Greens</u>

Serves: 2

Nutritional values per serving: 1 ¼ cups
Calories: 200, Fat: 5.8 g, Cholesterol: 3.6 mg, Carbohydrates: 29 g, Fiber: 5.9 g, Protein: 8.6 g

Ingredients:
- 1 can (14 ounces) low-sodium, hearty-style, tomato soup
- 1 ½ cups chopped kale
- crushed red pepper to taste
- salt to taste
- ⅛ cup grated low-fat Parmesan cheese
- ½ tablespoon olive oil
- ½ teaspoon minced garlic
- ½ can (from a 15 ounces can) unsalted cannellini beans, drained, rinsed

Directions:

1. Warm up the soup in a pan.

2. Pour oil into a skillet and let it heat over medium heat. When the oil is hot, add kale and stir. Cook for a couple of minutes until kale turns limp.
3. Add garlic and crushed red pepper and stir constantly for a few seconds, taking care not to burn the red pepper.
4. Add the kale into the pan of warm soup. Add beans as well. Mix well and heat thoroughly.
5. Ladle into soup bowls. Garnish with Parmesan and serve.

Lentil Vegetable Soup

Serves: 4–5

Nutritional values per serving: ¼ recipe
Calories: 278, Fat: 5.2 g, Cholesterol: 11 mg, Carbohydrates: 40.5 g, Fiber: 8.7 g, Protein: 15.4 g

Ingredients:
- ½ pound dry French green lentils, soaked in boiling water for 30–60 minutes
- 2 cups leeks, white parts only
- 2 cups chopped onions
- ½ tablespoon minced garlic
- salt to taste
- 2 carrots, chopped
- 4 stalks celery, chopped
- ½ tablespoon Kosher salt or to taste
- 6 cups chicken stock
- freshly ground black pepper to taste
- ½ teaspoon ground cumin
- 2 tablespoons tomato paste
- 1 tablespoon red wine or red wine vinegar
- ½ tablespoon chopped fresh thyme leaves, or ½ teaspoon dried thyme

Directions:

1. Pour oil into a soup pot and let it heat over medium heat. When the oil is hot, add onion, garlic, and leeks and cook for a couple of minutes.
2. Add thyme and cumin and sauté until the vegetables are slightly soft.
3. Add celery, lentils, carrots, and stock. When it begins to boil, turn down the heat to medium-low heat and cook until the lentils are tender. Add tomato paste and salt and cook for a few more minutes.
4. Stir in red wine.
5. Ladle into soup bowls and serve.

White Bean and Kale Soup

Serves: 3

Nutritional values per serving: ⅓ recipe
Calories: 237, Fat: 5 g, Cholesterol: 0 mg, Carbohydrates: 42 g, Fiber: 12 g, Protein: 14 g

Ingredients:
- 1 tablespoon olive oil
- 1 large carrot, diced
- ½ stalk celery, diced
- 1 teaspoon Italian seasoning
- ½ tablespoon tomato paste
- 2 cups vegetable broth or chicken stock
- 2 cloves garlic, pressed
- ½ onion, finely chopped
- 1 bay leaf
- 1 ½ cans (15 ounces each) cannellini beans, drained, rinsed
- 1 cup chopped baby kale or spinach
- salt to taste
- pepper to taste

Directions:

1. Pour oil into a soup pot and let it heat over medium-high heat. When the oil is hot, add onion and garlic and stir. Cook for a few minutes until the onion is pink.
2. Stir in celery and carrots and cook for a couple of minutes.
3. Add tomato paste, beans, salt, pepper, bay leaf, and Italian seasoning and mix well.
4. Add broth and stir. When the soup starts boiling, turn down the heat to low heat and cook until the vegetables are tender.
5. Blend some of the beans with an immersion blender or in a blender until smooth. Add the blended soup back into the pot.
6. Stir in the kale and cook for a few minutes until the kale turns limp and bright green in color.
7. Ladle into soup bowls and serve.

Rosemary Garlic Bean Soup

Serves: 2–3

Nutritional values per serving: 1 ¼ cups
Calories: 180, Fat: 8.2 g, Cholesterol: 0 mg, Carbohydrates: 61.91 g, Fiber: 17.05 g, Protein: 14.2 g

Ingredients:
- 1 tablespoon olive oil
- 2 cans mixed beans (15 ounces each)
- ⅛ teaspoon dried thyme
- ¼ teaspoon dried rosemary
- freshly cracked pepper to taste
- 2 cloves garlic, minced
- 1 cup vegetable or chicken broth
- ¼ teaspoon crushed red pepper

Directions:

1. Blend one can of beans along with the liquid in a blender until smooth.
2. Drain off the liquid from the other can of beans.

3. Pour oil into a soup pot and let it heat over medium heat. When the oil is hot, add garlic and cook for about a minute until light brown. Make sure you do not burn the garlic.
4. Stir in beans, blended beans, herbs, crushed red pepper, and broth.
5. When the soup starts boiling, reduce the heat to medium-low heat and cook for about 10 minutes. Stir occasionally.
6. Taste a bit of the soup and add salt if required.
7. Ladle into soup bowls and serve.

Vegan "Beef" Stew

Serves: 4

Nutritional values per serving: ¼ recipe
Calories: 196, Fat: 7 g, Cholesterol: 0 mg, Carbohydrates: 25 g, Fiber: 7 g, Protein: 8 g

Ingredients:
- 1 ½ tablespoons vegetable oil
- ⅛ cup all-purpose flour
- ½ teaspoon pepper or to taste
- 1 medium carrot, finely chopped
- 2 cloves garlic, minced
- ½ large onion, diced
- 1 ½ stalks celery, finely chopped
- 2 medium potatoes, peeled, chopped into bite size pieces
- 1 ⅛ cups TVP (textured vegetable protein)
- 1 tablespoon mixed dried herbs of your choice
- ¼ cup red wine (optional)
- 1 tablespoon soy sauce or tamari
- 1 tablespoon chopped fresh parsley to garnish
- 2 cups vegetable stock
- salt to taste
- ½ tablespoon vegan butter (optional but recommended)

Directions:
1. Pour boiling water over TVP in a bowl. Let it soak for 20 minutes. Drain in a colander and squeeze out water from the TVP.
2. Place it back in the bowl. Sprinkle flour, salt, pepper, and half the mixed dried herbs and toss well.
3. Pour 1 tablespoon of oil into a pot and let it heat over medium heat. When oil is hot, add TVP and cook until brown all over. Remove them onto a plate.
4. Pour remaining oil into the pot. When oil is hot, add carrots, onion, garlic, and celery and stir. Turn down the heat to medium-low heat. Cook for a couple of minutes.
5. Add salt and pepper to taste. Let it cook for another 2 minutes.
6. Add mixed dried herbs and wine if using. Let it cook for a few minutes until most of the wine has gone.
7. Stir in potatoes, soy sauce, TVP, and stock.
8. Cook covered until the potatoes are cooked and the stew is thickened to your preference.
9. Taste the stew and add more salt and pepper if required. Add vegan butter and stir.
10. Sprinkle parsley on top and serve.

Tunisian Fish and Vegetable Stew

Serves: 8

Nutritional values per serving: ⅛ recipe
Calories: 509, Fat: 24 g, Cholesterol: 124 mg, Carbohydrates: 32.9 g, Fiber: 5.2 g, Protein: 41.7 g

Ingredients:
- 1 ½ tablespoons olive oil
- 8 cloves garlic, thinly sliced
- 3 teaspoons ground cumin
- 1 teaspoon freshly ground pepper or to taste
- 6 cups chicken stock or broth
- 6 tablespoons tomato paste
- 6 carrots, peeled, cut into 1 inch pieces
- 4 zucchini, cut into 1 inch pieces
- 1 ½ pounds boiling potatoes, cut into 1 inch cubes
- 2 turnips, cut into 1 inch pieces
- 3 pounds cod filets, cut into 1 ½ inch pieces
- ½ teaspoon red pepper flakes to taste
- 2 teaspoons salt
- ⅓ cup chopped fresh parsley to garnish

Directions:
1. Pour oil into a large pot and let it heat over medium heat. When the oil is hot, add garlic and onion and cook until onions are pink.
2. Stir in the broth, potatoes, and carrots. Let it cook for about 10 minutes.
3. Add tomato paste, salt, pepper, cumin, and red pepper flakes and mix well.
4. Let it cook for about 2 minutes. Add turnip and cook for another 10 minutes. Now add cod and stir. Cook for about 5–8 minutes or until the cod just cooks through.
5. Mix well. Garnish with parsley and serve.

Chicken and White Bean Stew

Serves: 3

Nutritional values per serving: 1 ¼ cups
Calories: 493, Fat: 10.9 g, Cholesterol: 67.8 mg, Carbohydrates: 53.8 g, Fiber: 27.4 g, Protein: 44.2 g

Ingredients:
- ½ pound dried cannellini beans, rinsed, soaked in water overnight, drained
- ½ cup chopped onion
- ½ teaspoon minced rosemary
- 1 pound bone-in chicken breast
- ½ tablespoon lemon juice
- ¼ teaspoon pepper
- ⅛ cup chopped flat-leaf parsley
- 3 cups unsalted chicken broth
- ½ cup sliced carrots
- 2 ounces Parmesan cheese rind

- ⅓ cup grated Parmesan cheese
- 2 cups chopped kale
- ¼ teaspoon Kosher salt
- 1 tablespoon extra-virgin olive oil

Directions:
1. If you have an instant pot or pressure cooker, go ahead and prepare in it. It will cook much faster. You can also make it in a slow cooker.
2. Add chicken, beans, onion, rosemary, broth, carrots, and Parmesan rind in a pot.
3. Place the pot over high heat. When the mixture starts boiling, turn down the heat and cook until the beans and chicken are tender.
4. Take out the chicken from the pot and place on your cutting board. When cool enough to handle, shred the chicken with a pair of forks and add it back into the pot.
5. Add kale and continue cooking for about 5 minutes or until kale wilts.
6. Add oil and stir. Serve in bowls topped with Parmesan and parsley.

Middle Eastern Chicken and Chickpea Stew

Serves: 8

Nutritional values per serving: 1 ¼ cups
Calories: 267, Fat: 7.9 g, Cholesterol: 62.7 mg, Carbohydrates: 21.5 g, Fiber: 5.7 g, Protein: 28.2 g

Ingredients:
- 8 cloves garlic, minced
- ½ cup lemon juice
- 2 teaspoons paprika
- 2 pounds boneless, skinless chicken breasts, trimmed, cut into 1 inch pieces
- 2 large yellow onions, chopped
- 2 cans (15 ounces each) chickpeas, drained, rinsed
- 1 ½ teaspoons salt, divided
- 2 teaspoons ground cumin
- 1 teaspoon pepper
- 2 tablespoons extra-virgin olive oil
- 2 cans (14 ounces each) unsalted diced tomatoes with its juice
- ½ cup chopped flat-leaf parsley

Directions:
1. Place garlic and a teaspoon of salt together on your cutting board. Smash it up well using a back of fork.
2. Add the smashed garlic into a big bowl. Add lemon juice, pepper, paprika, and cumin and mix well.
3. Add chicken and mix well.
4. Pour oil into a large cast-iron skillet and let it heat over medium-high heat. When the oil is hot, add onion and cook until caramelized. Stir occasionally.
5. Take out the chicken from the bowl with a slotted spoon and add into the pan. Do not discard the marinade.
6. Sear the chicken for about 2 minutes on each side. Stir in tomatoes, ½ teaspoon salt, chickpeas and retained marinade.
7. Turn down the heat to medium-low heat and simmer until the chicken is well-cooked inside.
8. Garnish with parsley and serve.

Chapter 7: Salads

Making a salad is as simple as cooking can get! The different salad recipes given in this chapter are tasty and can be tossed together in no time.

Mediterranean Three Bean Salad

Serves: 3

Nutritional values per serving: ⅓ recipe
Calories: 295, Fat: 5.6 g, Cholesterol: 0 mg, Carbohydrates: 48.43 g, Fiber: 15.8 g, Protein: 15.8 g

Ingredients:
For salad:
- ½ can (from a 15 ounces can) dark red kidney beans, drained, rinsed
- ½ can (from a 15 ounces can) black beans, drained, rinsed
- ½ can (from a 15 ounces can) butter beans, drained, rinsed
- ½ cup corn kernels
- ½ small onion, chopped
- ½ cup chopped cucumber
- ½ large tomato chopped
- ¼ green bell pepper, chopped
- ½ cup chopped parsley or cilantro

For dressing:
- 2 tablespoons extra-virgin olive oil
- 1 clove garlic, minced
- juice of ½ lemon
- ¼ teaspoon salt or to taste
- ¼ teaspoon ground cumin
- ¼ teaspoon pepper or to taste

Directions:

1. To make dressing: Whisk together oil, garlic, lemon juice, and seasonings in a bowl.
2. Add corn, onion, tomato, cucumber, bell pepper, parsley, and all the beans into a bowl and toss well.
3. Add dressing and mix well.
4. Let the salad rest for 30 minutes for the flavors to meld.
5. Toss well and serve.

Kachumar Salad

Serves: 4

Nutritional values per serving: ¼ recipe
Calories: 30, Fat: 0.23 g, Cholesterol: 0 mg, Carbohydrates: 6.8 g, Fiber: 1.7 g, Protein: 1 g

Ingredients:
- 1 cucumber, peeled, finely chopped
- 1 onion, finely chopped
- 1 tomato, finely chopped
- 1 carrot, finely chopped
- juice of ½ lemon
- salt to taste
- 1 green chili, split
- ¼ cup chopped cilantro

Directions:

1. Place cucumber, onion, tomato, carrot, salt, lemon juice, green chili, and cilantro in a bowl and mix well.
2. Cover and set aside for a while for the flavors to blend.
3. Mix well and serve.

Carrot Salad

Serves: 4

Nutritional values per serving: ¼ recipe
Calories: 143, Fat: 9.3 g, Cholesterol: 0 mg, Carbohydrates: 12 g, Fiber: 4.2 g, Protein: 5.9 g

Ingredients:
- 4 carrots, grated
- 2 tomatoes, chopped
- juice of a lemon
- ½ cup roasted peanuts, crushed
- 2 green chilies, split
- ½ teaspoon salt

Directions:

1. Combine carrots, tomatoes, lemon juice, green chilies, salt, and peanuts in a bowl.
2. Let the salad sit on your countertop for about 30 minutes.
3. Mix well and serve.

Beetroot Salad

Serves: 4

Nutritional values per serving: ¼ recipe
Calories: 47, Fat: 0.25 g, Cholesterol: 0 mg, Carbohydrates: 11 g, Fiber: 2.2 g, Protein: 1.7 g

Ingredients:
- 4 medium beets, boiled, peeled, halved, thinly sliced
- 1 large tomato, diced
- 2 small onions, halved, thinly sliced
- 2 green chilies, split
- juice of a lemon
- ½ teaspoon salt
- ¼ cup chopped cilantro

Directions:

1. Combine beets, tomato, onions, green chilies, lemon juice, salt, and cilantro in a bowl.
2. Cover and set aside for about 30 minutes.
3. Mix well and serve.

Veggie Salad

Serves: 4

Nutritional values per serving: ¼ recipe
Calories: 174, Fat: 8.11 g, Cholesterol: 0 mg, Carbohydrates: 21.4 g, Fiber: 5.6 g, Protein: 8.1 g

Ingredients:
For salad:
- 4 cups shredded cabbage
- 1 tomato, chopped
- 1 carrot, halved lengthwise, thinly sliced
- 1 red radish, halved, thinly sliced

- 1 head lettuce, shredded
- ¼ cup roasted peanuts

For dressing:
- 1 tablespoon white vinegar
- ½ teaspoon sugar or honey
- ¼ teaspoon salt
- ¼ teaspoon pepper
- ¼ teaspoon red pepper flakes
- 1 tablespoon extra-virgin olive oil
- 1 clove garlic, minced

Directions:

1. To make dressing: Whisk together vinegar, sugar, seasonings, oil, and garlic in a bowl. Set aside for about 30 minutes for the flavors to meld.
2. To make salad: Combine cabbage, tomato, carrot, radish, and lettuce in a bowl.
3. Chill until use.
4. Add dressing and peanuts and toss well.

Mediterranean Couscous Salad

Serves: 3

Nutritional values per serving: ⅓ recipe
Calories: 378, Fat: 23.61 g, Cholesterol: 93 mg, Carbohydrates: 17.8 g, Fiber: 2.7 g, Protein: 23.7 g

Ingredients:
For couscous:
- ½ cup instant couscous
- 1 tablespoon extra-virgin olive oil
- ½ cup water
- ¼ teaspoon Kosher salt

For salad:
- ¼ cup diced Roma tomato
- ¼ cup diced red bell pepper
- 1 small onion, diced
- ¼ cup diced English cucumber
- ¼ cup canned or cooked chickpeas, rinsed, drained
- ¼ cup kalamata olive, pitted, sliced
- 1 tablespoon chopped parsley
- 1 tablespoon fresh basil
- 1 tablespoon chopped fresh mint
- ⅛ teaspoon dried oregano
- 1 tablespoon crumbled feta cheese

For lemon dressing:
- ½ teaspoon grated lemon zest
- ½ tablespoon red wine vinegar

- pepper to taste
- 1 tablespoon lemon juice
- ⅛ teaspoon Kosher salt or to taste
- 1 ½ tablespoons extra-virgin olive oil

Directions:

1. Combine salt, oil, and water in a saucepan. Place the saucepan over medium heat.
2. When water starts boiling, stir in the couscous and remove from heat.
3. Cover the saucepan and let it rest for 5 minutes.
4. Using a fork, fluff the grains. Let it cool completely. You can spread the couscous on a baking sheet to cool.
5. To make salad: Place couscous in a large bowl. Add cucumber, chickpeas, olives, mint, parsley, oregano, basil, onion, and feta cheese and toss well.
6. To make lemon dressing: Add lemon juice, lemon zest, vinegar, pepper, and salt into a small bowl. Whisk until well combined.
7. Whisking constantly, pour oil in a thin drizzle. Keep whisking until the dressing is slightly emulsified.
8. Add dressing over the salad. Toss well and serve.

Quinoa Salad

Serves: 2–3

Nutritional values per serving: ¾ cup
Calories: 227, Fat: 12 g, Cholesterol: 0 mg, Carbohydrates: 25 g, Fiber: 3 g, Protein: 5 g

Ingredients:
- ¾ cup quinoa, rinsed, drained
- 3 tablespoons olive oil, divided
- 2 tablespoons lemon juice
- 3 tablespoons minced fresh mint leaves
- 3 tablespoons minced fresh parsley
- ¾ teaspoon salt
- 1 mini cucumber, sliced
- ¼ cup chopped red onion
- 1 ½ cups water
- ½ tablespoon grated lemon zest
- 2 cloves garlic, minced
- ½ cup cherry tomatoes, halved
- ½ medium red bell pepper, chopped

Directions:

1. Add quinoa into a saucepan and place the saucepan over medium-high heat. Toast the quinoa for about 3 minutes, stirring often.
2. Stir in the water. When it starts boiling, turn down the heat to low heat and cook covered until dry and quinoa is tender. Turn off the heat.
3. Fluff the grains with a fork and add into a bowl. Let it cool for about 10–15 minutes.
4. To make dressing: Add oil, lemon juice, lemon zest, salt, garlic, and herbs into a bowl and whisk well.

5. Add vegetables to the bowl of quinoa. Pour dressing and mix well.
6. Cover the bowl and chill until use.
7. Mix well once again and serve.

Caribbean Couscous Salad

Serves: 4–5

Nutritional values per serving: ⅔ cup
Calories: 156, Fat: 3.4 g, Cholesterol: 0 mg, Carbohydrates: 28.9 g, Fiber: 5.7 g, Protein: 6.4 g

Ingredients:
- ⅛ cup chopped cilantro
- 1 tablespoon canola oil
- ¼ teaspoon salt
- ½ cup + ⅛ cup water
- ½ can (from a 15 ounces can) black beans, drained, rinsed
- ½ medium red bell pepper, chopped
- ⅛ cup thinly sliced scallion
- 1 ½ tablespoons lime juice
- ¾ teaspoon grated fresh ginger
- cayenne pepper to taste
- ½ cup whole-wheat couscous
- 1 cup shredded fresh spinach
- ½ medium mango, peeled, chopped

Directions:

1. To make dressing: Add lime juice, ginger, cayenne, salt, oil, and cilantro into a bowl and whisk well.
2. Set it aside for a while for the flavors to blend.
3. Meanwhile, boil water in a small saucepan. Turn off the heat. Add couscous and stir.
4. Cover the saucepan and let it rest for 5 minutes.
5. Using a fork, fluff the grains. Let it cool for 10–15 minutes.
6. Add beans, spinach, mango, couscous, bell pepper, and scallion into a bowl.
7. Pour dressing over the salad. Mix well and serve. You can serve it right away or chill and serve later.

Warm Sumac Fish and Quinoa Salad

Serves: 4

Nutritional values per serving: ¼ recipe
Calories: 504, Fat: 24.5 g, Cholesterol: 79 mg, Carbohydrates: 33.8 g, Fiber: 3.8 g, Protein: 36.2 g

Ingredients:
- 1 large onion, chopped
- 1 medium zucchini, cut into slices on the diagonal
- ½ cup chopped fresh mint leaves
- 2 cloves garlic, crushed

- 1 cup halved cherry tomatoes
- 1 ½ cups vegetable stock
- 1.4 pounds firm white fish filets
- 1 cup quinoa
- 4 teaspoons sumac
- salt to taste
- 3–4 tablespoons lemon juice
- 2 tablespoons olive oil

Directions:

1. Pour oil into a pan and let it heat over medium heat. Add onion and cook for a minute.
2. Add zucchini and tomatoes. Mix well and cook for about 5 minutes or until vegetables are tender. Turn off the heat.
3. Meanwhile, boil stock in a saucepan over medium heat. Add quinoa and stir. When it starts boiling, turn down the heat to low heat and cook covered until dry.
4. Turn off the heat and let it rest for 5 minutes. Uncover and fluff the grains with a fork. Let it cool until the fish is grilled.
5. Sprinkle sumac over the fish. Grill the fish on a preheated grill for about 6–7 minutes on each side or until it flakes easily when pierced with a fork.
6. Add cooked vegetables, mint leaves and lemon juice to the bowl of quinoa. Add salt to taste. Mix well and serve warm topped with fish.

Chapter 8: Chicken Recipes

Lean poultry plays an important role in improving cholesterol levels. Get your daily dose of protein by using the tasty recipes in this chapter.

Asian Chicken Lettuce Wraps

Serves: 2

Nutritional values per serving: 2 wraps
Calories: 265, Fat: 9.3 g, Cholesterol: 99 mg, Carbohydrates: 3.3 g, Fiber: 1 g, Protein: 40.7 g

Ingredients:
- ½ tablespoon canola oil
- ½ tablespoon rice vinegar
- ¾ teaspoon chili garlic sauce
- ¼ teaspoon grated orange rind
- pinch sea salt
- 4 Boston lettuce leaves
- ¼ cup bean sprouts
- roasted, chopped peanuts to garnish
- ½ tablespoon dark sesame oil
- ½ tablespoon soy sauce

- ½ teaspoon grated fresh ginger
- 1 clove garlic, minced
- 2 chicken breast halves (6 ounces each)
- ½ cup fresh mint leaves
- lime wedges to serve

Directions:

1. Combine canola oil, sesame oil, vinegar, soy sauce, chili garlic sauce, ginger, orange rind, garlic, and salt in a bowl.
2. Remove a tablespoonful or two of the marinade and keep it aside in a bowl.
3. Add chicken into a Ziploc bag. Pour the remaining marinade into the bag. Seal the bag and turn it around a few times so that chicken is well coated with the marinade.
4. Place a nonstick pan over medium-high heat. Spray some cooking spray into the pan. Take out only the chicken from the bag and place it in the bag. The marinade is to be discarded.
5. Cook for about 6 minutes on each side or until cooked through inside. Turn off the heat.
6. Take out the chicken from the pan and place on your cutting board. When the chicken cools slightly, cut into thin slices.
7. To assemble: Place lettuce leaves on a serving platter. Distribute the chicken slices among the lettuce leaves. Divide equally the mint and beansprouts among the leaves. Drizzle retained marinade on top and serve garnished with peanuts and lime wedges.

Chicken and Broccoli Quinoa

Serves: 3

Nutritional values per serving: ⅓ recipe
Calories: 409.1, Fat: 9.1 g, Cholesterol: 73.3 mg, Carbohydrates: 38.8 g, Fiber: 6.3 g, Protein: 43.3 g

Ingredients:
For chicken:
- 1 pound boneless, skinless chicken breasts, cut into 1 inch pieces
- ¼ teaspoon ground cumin
- ¼ teaspoon Himalayan pink salt
- ½ tablespoon extra-virgin olive oil
- ¼ teaspoon ground allspice (optional but recommended)
- pepper to taste

For quinoa:
- 1 medium onion, diced
- ½ large carrot, shredded
- ¾ cup uncooked quinoa
- ½ teaspoon Himalayan pink salt or to taste
- 1 bay leaf
- 1 ½ large cloves garlic, minced
- ½ teaspoon extra-virgin olive oil
- 1 ½ cups boiling water
- ¼ teaspoon ground cumin
- ½ pound broccoli, chopped

Directions:

1. To cook chicken: Heat a heavy pot over medium-high heat. When the pan is hot, add chicken, salt, cumin, oil, allspice, and pepper and mix well.
2. Cook until the chicken is slightly golden brown. Remove chicken onto a plate.
3. To make quinoa: Pour oil into the same pot. When the oil is hot, add onion and garlic and cook for a couple of minutes. Stir in the carrots. Cook for another 2 to 3 minutes.
4. Stir in chicken, water, quinoa, salt if desired, bay leaf, and cumin. When the mixture starts boiling, turn down the heat to low heat and cook until very little water is remaining in the pot.
5. Stir in the broccoli. Continue cooking covered until dry. Turn off the heat and let it rest for 5 minutes.
6. Uncover and fluff the quinoa and vegetables with a fork.
7. Serve hot.

Grilled Chicken and Sweet Potato Packets

Serves: 3

Nutritional values per serving: 1 ⅓ cups
Calories: 241, Fat: 2.6 g, Cholesterol: 55.2 mg, Carbohydrates: 33.8 g, Fiber: 6.8 g, Protein: 20.5 g

Ingredients:
- ½ pound boneless, skinless chicken breast, cut into 1 inch pieces
- 2 ½ cups diced red bell peppers
- 2 small cloves garlic, sliced
- 2 ½ cups peeled, cubed sweet potatoes
- ½ large red onion, sliced
- ½ teaspoon salt
- ¼ teaspoon ground cumin
- lime wedges to serve
- ½ teaspoon chili powder
- ¼ teaspoon dried oregano

Directions:

1. Set up your grill and preheat it to medium-high heat.
2. Take three sheets of heavy duty foil for about 12 inches each. Spray some cooking spray on each foil.
3. Add chicken, bell pepper, garlic, onion, and sweet potato into a bowl and mix well.
4. Distribute equally the mixture and place on the foil. Now wrap the foils to make packets.
5. Place the packets on the grill and cook for about 20 minutes or until chicken and sweet potato is cooked. Turn the packets over after cooking for about 10 minutes.
6. Serve. You need to be careful when you open the packets as steam from the packets can gush out.
7. Serve each packet with a lime wedge.

BBQ Chicken Tenders

Serves: 4–5

Nutritional values per serving: 1 tender
Calories: 69, Fat: 0.7 g, Cholesterol: 24.2 mg, Carbohydrates: 7.8 g, Fiber: 0.6 g, Protein: 8.1 g

Ingredients:
- ½ cup BBQ sauce
- 1 tablespoon honey
- ¼ cup all-purpose flour
- ¼ teaspoon freshly ground pepper
- ¾ cup + ⅛ cup whole-wheat breadcrumbs
- 1 tablespoon Dijon mustard
- ¾ pound chicken tenders
- ¼ teaspoon salt
- 1 large egg

Directions:

1. Add BBQ sauce, honey, and mustard into a bowl and stir.
2. Remove about ¼ cup of the sauce mixture and keep it aside for now.
3. If there are any large pieces of chicken tenders cut into two halves lengthwise.
4. Place chicken tenders in the bowl with remaining sauce mixture. Turn it over a few times so that chicken is well coated with the sauce mixture. Place the bowl covered in the refrigerator for 30–60 minutes.
5. Preheat the oven to 450°F. Prepare a rimmed baking sheet by spraying it with cooking spray.
6. Place salt, pepper, and flour in a shallow bowl and stir well.
7. Crack the egg into a shallow bowl and beat well.
8. Put the breadcrumbs on a plate or shallow bowl.
9. First dredge the chicken tenders, one at a time in flour. Shake off extra flour and dunk in egg. Shake off extra egg and finally dredge in breadcrumbs.
10. Keep the tenders on the baking sheet.
11. Spray some cooking spray on either side of the chicken tenders.
12. Place the baking sheet in the oven and set the timer for 20 minutes. Flip sides after about 10 minutes. Cook until crispy on top and well-cooked inside.
13. Serve with the sauce that was set aside.

Szechuan Chicken Stir-Fry

Serves: 4

Nutritional values per serving: ¼ recipe
Calories: 420, Fat: 16.7 g, Cholesterol: 66 mg, Carbohydrates: 32.3 g, Fiber: 2.7 g, Protein: 32.3 g

Ingredients:
- 1 ½ teaspoons dark sesame oil, divided
- 1 tablespoon soy sauce
- 1 teaspoon chili paste

- ⅛ teaspoon salt or to taste
- ¼ cup fat-free chicken broth
- ½ tablespoon rice vinegar
- 1 teaspoon cornstarch
- 1 tablespoon canola oil, divided
- ½ red bell pepper, cut into strips
- ½ yellow bell pepper, cut into strips
- ½ cup snow peas, cut on the bias
- ½ tablespoon grated ginger
- 1 cup hot cooked long grain brown rice
- ⅛ cup roasted, unsalted peanuts
- ½ pound skinless, boneless chicken breast halves, cut into bite size chunks
- 1 small onion, halved, thinly sliced
- ½ tablespoon minced garlic
- 1 green onion, cut into 1 inch pieces

Directions:

1. Add 1 teaspoon sesame oil, soy sauce, chili paste, salt, broth, vinegar, and cornstarch in a bowl and whisk well.
2. Pour ½ tablespoon canola oil and ½ teaspoon oil into a wok or pan and place it over medium-high heat.
3. When the oil is hot, add chicken and cook for a couple of minutes. Transfer the chicken into a bowl.
4. Pour ½ tablespoon of canola oil into the wok. When the oil is hot, add bell peppers, snow peas, onion, garlic, and ginger and stir often for about a minute.
5. Stir in the sauce mixture. Keep stirring until the sauce thickens.
6. Add the chicken and mix well. Let it cook until the chicken is well-cooked inside.
7. To assemble: Serve rice on plates. Divide the chicken and sauce equally and spoon over the rice. Garnish with peanuts and green onion and serve.

Chicken Sausage and Broccoli Rabe Penne

Serves: 2

Nutritional values per serving: ½ recipe
Calories: 374, Fat: 12 g, Cholesterol: 58 mg, Carbohydrates: 48 g, Fiber: 6 g, Protein: 25 g

Ingredients:
- 4 ounces uncooked multigrain penne pasta
- ½ tablespoon olive oil
- ¼ teaspoon freshly ground black pepper
- ¾ tablespoon fresh lemon juice
- 4 cups water
- ½ pound broccoli rabe, trimmed, chopped
- 1 smoked chicken sausage (3 ounces), cut on the bias into 8 pieces
- Kosher salt to taste
- 1 ounce Pecorino Romano cheese, grated

Directions:

1. Pour water into a saucepan and place it over high heat. When it starts boiling, add pasta and let it cook for 7 minutes.
2. Next drop the broccoli rabe into the saucepan. Drain off after 2 minutes but retain about ⅓ cup of the cooked liquid.
3. Pour oil into a skillet and let it heat over medium heat. When the oil is hot, add sausage and cook until brown on each side.
4. Add pasta, salt, pepper, and retained pasta cooked water. Mix well. Cook for a couple of minutes until nearly dry.
5. Add lemon juice and stir. Turn off the heat.
6. Serve in bowls garnished with cheese.

Chicken and Apple Kale Wraps

Serves: 2

Nutritional values per serving: 3 wraps
Calories: 370, Fat: 13.7 g, Cholesterol: 78.1 mg, Carbohydrates: 34.1 g, Fiber: 6 g, Protein: 29.3 g

Ingredients:
- 2 tablespoons mayonnaise (preferably egg white mayonnaise)
- 6 medium lacinato kale leaves
- 12 thin red onion slices
- 2 teaspoons Dijon mustard
- 6 ounces thinly sliced cooked chicken breast
- 2 firm apples, cored, cut each into 9 slices

Directions:

1. Add mustard and mayonnaise into a bowl and mix well.
2. Place kale leaves on a serving platter. Spread the mayonnaise mixture over the kale leaves
3. Divide the chicken among the leaves. Place two onion slices on each leaf followed by three apple slices.
4. Roll the leaves and place with its seam side facing down.
5. Serve.

Avocado, Tomato, and Chicken Sandwich

Serves: 2

Nutritional values per serving: 1 sandwich
Calories: 347, Fat: 12.3 g, Cholesterol: 62.7mg, Carbohydrates: 28.4 g, Fiber: 7.7 g, Protein: 31.2 g,

Ingredients:
- 4 slices multigrain bread, toasted
- 6 ounces cooked, boneless, skinless chicken breast, cut into slices
- ½ ripe avocado, peeled, pitted, mashed
- 4 thin, round tomato slices

Directions:

1. Spread avocado on the bread slices. Divide equally the chicken and tomato slices and place on two bread slices, over the avocado.
2. Cover with the remaining two bread slices, with the avocado side facing down.
3. Cut into the desired shape and serve.

Chapter 9: Vegetarian and Vegan

Increasing the intake of plant-based foods is one of the best dietary changes anyone can make. So, use the delicious vegetarian and vegan recipes in this chapter to get your daily dose of nutrients.

<u>Mushroom Bean Bourguignon</u>

Serves: 4–5

Nutritional values per serving: 1 cup
Calories: 234, Fat: 6 g, Cholesterol: 0 mg, Carbohydrates: 33 g, Fiber: 7 g, Protein: 9 g

Ingredients:
- 2 tablespoons olive oil, divided
- 1 medium onion, halved, sliced
- 4 large Portobello mushrooms, cut into 1 inch pieces
- 12.7 ounces dry red wine
- ½ teaspoon salt
- ¼ teaspoon pepper
- 2–3 medium carrots, cut into 1 inch chunks
- 1 clove garlic, minced
- ½ tablespoon tomato paste
- 1 cup mushroom broth or vegetable broth, divided
- ½ teaspoon minced fresh thyme or ¼ teaspoon dried thyme

- 1 can (from 15.5 ounces can) navy beans, rinsed, drained
- 1 ½ tablespoons all-purpose flour
- ¼ teaspoon pepper
- ½ package (from a 14.4 ounces package) frozen pearl onions

Directions:

1. Pour a tablespoon of oil into a heavy pot or Dutch oven and let it heat over medium-high heat.
2. When the oil is hot, add onion and cook for about a minute.
3. Stir in carrots and cook for a few minutes until the vegetables are slightly tender.
4. Stir in the garlic and cook for a few seconds until you get a nice aroma.
5. Transfer the mixture into a bowl. Pour 1 tablespoon of oil into the same pot. When the oil is hot, add mushrooms and cook until light brown.
6. Stir in the tomato paste. Cook for about a minute. Add the carrots, ¾ cup of broth, wine, and seasonings.
7. When it starts boiling, turn down the heat to low heat and cook covered for about 15 minutes.
8. Stir in the pearl onions and beans. Let the mixture simmer for about 20 minutes.
9. Whisk together flour and ¾ cup broth and pour into the pot. Stir constantly until thick.

Eggs on Beans

Serves: 2

Nutritional values per serving: ½ recipe
Calories: 281, Fat: 12.8 g, Cholesterol: 623 mg, Carbohydrates: 20.8 g, Fiber: 7.3 g, Protein: 22.43 g

Ingredients:
- ½ large brown onion, finely chopped
- ½ can (from 14 ounces can) chopped tomatoes
- 1–2 ripe tomatoes, diced
- 1.75 ounces canned or cooked red kidney beans, rinsed, drained
- 1.75 ounces canned or cooked black eyed beans, rinsed, drained
- 1.75 ounces canned or cooked cannellini beans, rinsed, drained
- chopped parsley to garnish
- ½ teaspoon smoked paprika
- ½ teaspoon ground black pepper
- ¼ teaspoon chili flakes
- ½ teaspoon cayenne pepper
- ½ teaspoon ground cumin
- ¼ teaspoon coarse sea salt
- 2 small cloves garlic, finely chopped
- 1 tablespoon tomato puree
- ¼ yellow bell pepper, sliced
- 2 eggs

Directions:

1. Preheat the oven to 350°F.

2. Pour oil into an ovenproof skillet and let it heat over medium heat. When the oil is hot, add onion and cook for a few minutes until it turns light brown. Add garlic and stir constantly for about a minute or until you get a nice aroma.

3. Add bell peppers, fresh tomatoes and canned tomatoes. Mix well and cook for a few minutes until the bell peppers and fresh tomatoes are slightly soft.

4. Add all the spices, salt, tomato puree, and beans and mix well. Cover and cook for about 5 minutes or until thick. Stir well.

5. Make two cavities in the sauce. Crack an egg into each cavity and turn off the oven.

6. Shift the skillet into the oven and set the timer for 8–9 minutes or until the whites are set and the yolks are runny. Once the timer goes off, take out the skillet and let it rest for 5 minutes on your countertop.

7. Uncover and garnish with parsley. Serve with multigrain bread.

Tofu Tacos

Nutritional values per serving: 2 tacos
Calories: 394, Fat: 17.9 g, Cholesterol: 0 mg, Carbohydrates: 18.8 g, Fiber: 10.1 g, Protein: 18.8 g

Ingredients:
- ½ tablespoon chili powder
- ¼ teaspoon dried oregano
- ⅛ teaspoon ground pepper
- ½ teaspoon ground cumin
- ¼ teaspoon salt or to taste
- ¼ teaspoon ground cinnamon
- 1 ½ tablespoons extra-virgin olive oil, divided
- 1 large clove garlic, minced
- 1 teaspoon cider vinegar
- 4 corn tortillas (warmed)
- 7–8 ounces block extra-firm tofu, dried with paper towels, cut into ½ inch cubes
- ¼ cup chopped onion
- ½ can (from a 15 ounces can) black beans, rinsed, drained
- ¼ cup chopped cilantro
- handful shredded cabbage
- toppings of your choice to serve

Directions:

1. Combine salt and seasonings in a bowl. Add tofu and mix well.

2. Pour 1 tablespoon of oil into a nonstick skillet and let it heat over medium heat. When the oil is hot, add onion and cook until translucent.

3. Stir in the garlic and cook for about a minute.

4. Turn up the heat to medium-high heat. Add tofu and mix well. Cook until light brown all over. Stir every now and then.

5. Stir in beans and cook for a couple of minutes. Turn off the heat. Add vinegar and cilantro and mix well.

6. Divide the tofu mixture equally and place over the tortillas. Place some cabbage on each tortilla. Also place toppings of your choice and serve.

Creamy Fettuccine With Brussels Sprouts and Mushrooms

Serves: 3

Nutritional values per serving: 1 ⅓ cups
Calories: 384, Fat: 10.2 g, Cholesterol: 20.7 mg, Carbohydrates: 56.4 g, Fiber: 9.6, Protein: 18.4 g

Ingredients:
- 6 ounces whole-wheat fettuccine pasta
- 2 cups sliced mixed mushrooms
- ½ tablespoon minced garlic
- 1 cup low-fat milk
- ¼ teaspoon salt
- ½ cup finely shredded Asiago cheese + extra to garnish if desired
- ½ tablespoon extra-virgin olive oil
- 2 cups thinly sliced Brussels sprouts
- ¼ cup dry sherry or 1 tablespoon sherry vinegar
- 1 tablespoon all-purpose flour
- ¼ teaspoon freshly ground pepper or to taste

Directions:

1. Follow the directions given on the package of pasta and cook the pasta. Add the drained pasta back into the pot and keep it aside.
2. Pour oil into a skillet and let it heat over medium heat. When the oil is hot, add mushrooms and Brussels sprouts and mix well. Cook until mushrooms are tender.
3. Stir in garlic and cook for a few seconds until you get a nice aroma. Stir in sherry. Scrape the bottom of the skillet to remove any browned bits that may be stuck.
4. Cook until nearly dry. Add milk, flour, salt, and pepper into a bowl and whisk well.
5. Pour the mixture into the skillet, stirring constantly. Keep stirring until thick and you can see bubbles around the edges of the skillet.
6. Add cheese and mix well. Add pasta and toss well. Garnish with some extra cheese if desired and serve.

Kung Pao Tofu

Serves: 4

Nutritional values per serving: ¼ recipe
Calories: 355, Fat: 22 g, Cholesterol: 0 mg, Carbohydrates: 26 g, Fiber: 9 g, Protein: 22 g

Ingredients:
For tofu and marinade:
- 2 pounds firm or extra-firm tofu, pressed of excess moisture, cut into bite size chunks
- 2 tablespoons fresh lime juice
- ⅓ cup vegetable broth
- 2 tablespoons sesame oil
- 4 tablespoons soy sauce

For stir-fry vegetables:
- 4 tablespoons sesame oil

- 2 red bell peppers, deseeded, diced
- 1 cup sliced mushrooms
- 2 small Bok Choy, chopped
- 1 cup snow peas
- 2 tablespoons chopped parsley
- salt to taste
- pepper to taste
- 2 onions, diced
- ½ teaspoon red pepper flakes
- 2 tablespoons fresh minced ginger
- ½ cup vegetable broth
- 2 teaspoons hot sauce
- 1 small purple cabbage, thinly sliced

Directions:

1. To make tofu: Whisk together broth, soy sauce, lime juice, and sesame oil in a bowl.
2. Add tofu and stir well. Let it marinate for 45–60 minutes. Stir every 15–20 minutes.
3. Preheat the oven to 375°F. Prepare a baking sheet by lining it with foil.
4. Remove the tofu from the marinade and place on the baking sheet.
5. Place the baking sheet in the oven and set the timer for 15 minutes.
6. Meanwhile, place a large pan or wok over medium-high heat. Add oil. When the oil is hot, add onions, mushrooms, and bell pepper and mix well. Cook until the onion turns pink.
7. Stir in ginger and red pepper flakes. Cook for a few seconds until you get a nice aroma.
8. Stir in Bok Choy and broth and cook for 5 minutes.
9. Turn down the heat to low heat. Add in the snow peas, cabbage, and tofu and mix well. Add salt, pepper, broth, parsley, and hot sauce and heat thoroughly.
10. Serve over hot cooked brown rice or quinoa or noodles.

Stuffed Eggplant with Couscous and Almonds

Serves: 2

Nutritional values per serving: 1 stuffed eggplant half with 2 tablespoons sauce
Calories: 457, Fat: 33 g, Cholesterol: 7.7 mg, Carbohydrates: 35.4 g, Fiber: 10.9 g, Protein: 9.2 g

Ingredients:
- ⅓ cup + ½ tablespoon water, divided
- ¼ teaspoon salt, divided
- 1 ½ tablespoons extra-virgin olive oil, divided
- 2 small cloves garlic, minced
- 1 teaspoon harissa paste or ¼ teaspoon harissa seasoning
- ¼ cup chopped fresh parsley
- ¼ cup whole-wheat couscous
- 1 medium eggplant (about a pound), halved lengthwise
- ⅛ teaspoon pepper
- 3 tablespoons mayonnaise
- ¼ cup roasted almonds, chopped

Directions:

1. Set up your grill and preheat it to medium-high heat.
2. Meanwhile, add ⅓ cup water, half the salt, and couscous into a saucepan. Place the saucepan over high heat. When the mixture starts boiling, turn off the heat. Cover the saucepan and let it rest.
3. Brush a tablespoon of oil on the cut part of the eggplant. Sprinkle a pinch of the remaining salt and pepper over the eggplant, on the cut part.
4. Place the eggplant halves on the grill and cook until charred on all the sides.
5. Take out the eggplant halves from the grill and let it cool for a few minutes.
6. Place garlic on your cutting board. Sprinkle remaining salt over the garlic and mash it well with the back of a fork.
7. Add mayonnaise, garlic, ½ tablespoon water and harissa into a small bowl and mix well.
8. Scoop out the eggplant pulp from the eggplant halves, leaving a border of ¼ inch near the peel. So you get eggplant shells.
9. Place the scooped eggplant in a bowl. Mash it up. Add almonds, couscous, ½ tablespoon oil, and parsley and mix well.
10. Fill up this mixture in the eggplant shells. Serve with mayonnaise sauce mixture.

Vegan Lentil and Mushroom Shepherd's Pie

Serves: 4

Nutritional values per serving: ¼ recipe
Calories: 359, Fat: 4.75 g, Cholesterol: 0 mg, Carbohydrates: 68.25 g, Fiber: 9.7 g, Protein: 2 g

Ingredients:
For mashed potatoes layer:
- 4 large or 5 medium Yukon gold potatoes, peeled, halved or quartered
- ¼ cup rice milk or any other non dairy milk of your choice
- pepper to taste
- 2 tablespoons vegan butter
- salt to taste

For the lentil layer:
- ½ large onion, chopped
- 3 ounces baby cremini mushrooms or baby Bella mushrooms
- 1 tablespoon dry red wine (optional)
- 1–2 teaspoons all-purpose seasoning blend
- 1 ½ tablespoons cornstarch or arrowroot mixed with 2–3 tablespoons water
- freshly ground pepper to taste
- 1 tablespoon olive oil
- 1 clove garlic, minced
- 1 can (15 ounces) lentils, slightly drained
- ½–1 tablespoon soy sauce or coconut aminos
- ¼ teaspoon dried thyme
- 4–5 ounces baby spinach or arugula
- ¼ cup fresh whole-wheat breadcrumbs
- salt to taste

Directions:

1. For mashed potato layer: Cook potatoes in a pot of water with salt added to it. Cook until soft. Drain well and transfer into a bowl.
2. Mash the potatoes with a potato masher until smooth. Add vegan butter, rice milk, salt and pepper. Cover and keep it aside.
3. Preheat the oven to 400°F.
4. Pour oil into a skillet and let it heat over medium heat. Add onions and cook for a few minutes until translucent. Add mushroom and garlic and stir. Cook until the mushroom turns golden brown.
5. Add lentils with some of its liquid, wine, thyme, seasoning blend, soy sauce, and thyme.
6. Cook covered for 5 minutes.
7. Add cornstarch mixture and stir constantly until thick. Stir in the spinach and cook until spinach wilts. Turn off the heat. Taste and adjust the seasoning if desired.
8. Grease a casserole dish or round baking dish with a little oil. Sprinkle breadcrumbs on the bottom of the dish.
9. Spread the lentil mixture over the breadcrumb layer.
10. Layer with the mashed potato evenly over the lentils.
11. Place the casserole dish in the oven and set the timer for 25–30 minutes or until golden brown on top.

Chapter 10: Fish and Seafood

Fish and seafood recipes given in this chapter are easy to cook and extremely delicious. Also, increasing the intake of these heart-healthy fats will lower cholesterol levels.

Shrimp Scampi

Serves: 2

Nutritional values per serving: ½ recipe
Calories: 341, Fat: 9 g, Cholesterol: 222 mg, Carbohydrates: 34 g, Fiber: 1 g, Protein: 29 g

Ingredients:
- ¾ pounds fresh or frozen large shrimp in shells, thawed if frozen, peeled, deveined (keep or leave the tails on), rinsed
- ½ tablespoon olive oil
- 1 tablespoon dry white wine or chicken broth
- salt to taste
- 3 ounces whole-wheat linguine
- 2 cloves garlic, minced
- ½ tablespoon butter
- ½ tablespoon chopped chives or parsley

Directions:

1. Dry the shrimp with paper towels.
2. Follow the directions given on the package of pasta and cook the pasta.
3. Keep it warm after draining.
4. Pour oil into a skillet and let it heat over medium-high heat. When the oil is hot, add garlic and cook for a few seconds until you get a nice aroma. Stir in the shrimp and cook until pink. Stir often.
5. Remove shrimp from the pan using a slotted spoon and place on a serving platter.
6. Pour wine into the skillet. Add salt and butter and stir. Scrape the bottom of the skillet to remove any browned bits that may be stuck.
7. Turn off the heat. Drizzle butter mixture over the shrimp. Garnish with chives.
8. Serve linguine on individual serving plates. Place shrimp on top and serve.

Shrimp and Scallop Vegetable Stir-Fry

Serves: 2

Nutritional values per serving: ½ recipe
Calories: 215, Fat: 1.9 g, Cholesterol: 67.2 mg, Carbohydrates: 32.3 g, Fiber: 5 g, Protein: 18.2 g

Ingredients:
- 4 ounces scallops, halved horizontally into discs
- 3 ounces medium shrimp, peeled, deveined
- ½ tablespoon soy sauce
- ¼ teaspoon ground ginger
- 2 cups small broccoli florets
- 1 teaspoon finely shredded ginger
- ½ cup shiitake mushrooms, discard stems, sliced
- ¾ cup hot cooked brown rice
- ¼ cup orange juice
- 1 teaspoon cornstarch
- crushed red pepper to taste
- ½ red bell pepper, cut into strips
- 2 small cloves garlic, minced

Directions:

1. Add soy sauce, orange juice, ground ginger, cornstarch, and red pepper flakes into a small bowl and stir.
2. Place a large nonstick pan over high heat. Spray some cooking spray into the pan. When the pan is hot, add bell pepper and broccoli and stir-fry for a couple of minutes until broccoli turns bright green in color.
3. Stir in shredded ginger and garlic. Keep stirring for a few seconds until you get a nice aroma. Stir in scallops, mushrooms, orange juice mixture, and shrimp.
4. Stir often for 3–4 minutes or until the seafood turns opaque and cooked as well.
5. Turn off the heat. Divide rice into two serving plates. Divide the stir-fry equally and spoon over the rice.

Shrimp Pad Thai

Serves: 2

Nutritional values per serving: ½ recipe
Calories: 462, Fat: 16.1 g, Cholesterol: 86 mg, Carbohydrates: 64.3 g, Fiber: 2.6 g, Protein: 15.8 g

Ingredients:
- 4 ounces flat brown rice noodles
- 1 tablespoon soy sauce
- ¾ tablespoon fresh lime juice
- 1 ½ tablespoons canola oil
- 4 ounces large shrimp, peeled, deveined
- ½ cup bean sprouts
- 1 ½ tablespoons fresh basil, chopped
- 1 tablespoon brown sugar
- ¾ tablespoon fish sauce
- ½ tablespoon Sriracha sauce or chili garlic sauce
- ½ cup green onion pieces (2 inch pieces)
- 3 cloves garlic, minced
- ⅛ cup roasted peanuts, unsalted

Directions:

1. Follow the directions given on the package of noodles and cook the noodles.
2. Combine brown sugar, soy sauce, fish sauce, lime juice, and Sriracha sauce in a bowl.
3. Pour oil into a wok or skillet and let it heat over medium-high heat. When oil is hot add onions, garlic and shrimp and mix well. Cook for a couple of minutes or until the shrimp is tender, stirring often.
4. Add noodles, mix well. Add the sauce mixture. Mix well.
5. To assemble: Divide the noodles into two serving bowls. Divide the bean sprouts, peanuts, and basil equally and place over the noodles.
6. Serve.

Herby Fish with Wilted Greens and Mushrooms

Serves: 2

Nutritional values per serving: 1 fish filet with ½ cup vegetables
Calories: 214, Fat: 11 g, Cholesterol: 45 mg, Carbohydrates: 11 g, Fiber: 3 g, Protein: 18 g

Ingredients:
- 1 ½ tablespoons olive oil, divided
- 1 ½ cups sliced cremini mushrooms
- 2 cups chopped kale
- 1 teaspoon Mediterranean herb mix or any other herb mix of your choice
- salt to taste
- 2 cods or tilapia or sole filets (6 ounces each)
- 1 medium sweet onion, sliced
- 1 clove garlic, sliced
- ½ medium tomato, diced

- ½ tablespoon lemon juice
- pepper to taste
- chopped fresh parsley to garnish

Directions:

1. Pour ½ tablespoon of oil into a saucepan and place it over medium heat. When the oil is hot, add onion and cook until it turns pink.
2. Stir in garlic and mushrooms and cook until mushrooms are slightly brown. Stir often.
3. Stir in kale, ½ teaspoon Mediterranean herb mix, and tomato. Cook for a few more minutes until mushrooms and kale is cooked. Add lemon juice, pepper, and salt to taste. Turn off the heat. Keep it warm until the fish is cooked.
4. Pour 1 tablespoon of oil into a nonstick skillet and let it heat over medium-high heat.
5. Sprinkle salt, ½ teaspoon herb mix, and pepper over the fish.
6. When the oil is hot, add fish and cook for 2–4 minutes on each side or cook until it turns opaque and flakes easily when pierced with a fork.

Lemon-Garlic Pasta with Salmon

Serves: 2

Nutritional values per serving: 1 ⅓ cups
Calories: 473, Fat: 23 g, Cholesterol: 25.5 mg, Carbohydrates: 49.4 g, Fiber: 5.9 g, Protein: 19.8 g

Ingredients:
- 4 ounces whole-wheat pasta
- 2–3 cloves garlic, chopped
- crushed red pepper to taste
- ¾ cup cooked, flaked salmon
- salt to taste
- 2 ½ tablespoons extra-virgin olive oil
- ½ teaspoon anchovy paste
- zest of ½ lemon, grated
- juice of ½ lemon
- 1–2 tablespoons chopped parsley
- 1 tablespoon whole-wheat breadcrumbs, toasted

Directions:
1. Follow the directions given on the package of pasta and cook the pasta.
2. Drain the pasta but retain about ¼ cup of the cooked water.
3. Place a skillet over medium-high heat. Add garlic, oil, red pepper, anchovy, lemon juice, and lemon zest.
4. When the mixture starts bubbling, stir in salmon, pasta, retained water, salt, and parsley. Mix well and let it cook for a couple of minutes. Garnish with breadcrumbs and serve.

Thai Coconut Fish Curry

Serves: 4

Nutritional values per serving: ¼ recipe
Calories: 344, Fat: 22.4 g, Cholesterol: 59 mg, Carbohydrates: 11.6 g, Fiber: 3.7 g, Protein: 25.3 g

Ingredients:
- 2 tablespoons olive oil or melted extra-virgin coconut oil
- 2 cloves garlic, minced
- ½ teaspoon finely grated lemon zest
- ¼ cup fish stock
- 1 teaspoon Thai green curry paste or more to taste
- 1 tablespoon fish sauce
- 1 cup canned, drained bamboo shoot strips
- ½ red bell pepper, diced
- toasted sesame seeds to garnish (optional)
- 1 onion, finely chopped
- ½ tablespoon minced ginger
- ½ cup vegetable stock
- 1 tablespoon fresh lime juice
- ½ cup light coconut milk
- 1 pound firm white fish, chopped into bite size pieces
- 1 cup frozen peas, thawed
- ¼ cup finely chopped fresh cilantro
- salt to taste

Directions:

1. Pour oil into a skillet and let it heat over medium heat. Add onions and cook until translucent. Stir in lime zest, ginger, and garlic. Cook for a few seconds until you get a nice aroma.
2. Add stock and stir. Cook for about 5 minutes
3. Combine lime juice, curry paste, fish sauce, and coconut milk in a cup. Pour this mixture into the skillet. Add bamboo shoots, green peas, and bell pepper.
4. Cook covered on medium-low heat until the fish is cooked and flakes readily when pierced with a fork.
5. Sprinkle cilantro and sesame seeds and serve over cooked brown rice.

Seasoned Cod

Serves: 4

Nutritional values per serving: ¼ recipe
Calories: 93, Fat: 0.7 g, Cholesterol: 48.3 mg, Carbohydrates: 0.1 g, Fiber: 0.1 g, Protein: 20.2 g

Ingredients:
- 1 pound fresh or frozen cod filets (¾–1 inch thick), thawed if frozen, rinsed
- ¼ teaspoon seasoned salt or more to taste
- ½ teaspoon paprika
- lemon wedges to serve
- fresh parsley sprigs to serve

Directions:

1. Set the oven to broil mode. Dry the fish by patting with paper towels.
2. Add paprika and seasoned salt into a bowl and mix well. Sprinkle this all over the filets.
3. Grease the rack of the broiler pan with some oil. Put the fish on the rack and place it 4 inches below the heating element.
4. Broil for 4–6 minutes on each side, depending on the thickness of the fish.
5. Serve garnished with parsley and lemon wedges.

Fish with Spicy Green Lentils

Serves: 2

Nutritional values per serving: ½ recipe
Calories: 372, Fat: 14 g, Cholesterol: 115 mg, Carbohydrates: 16 g, Fiber: 5 g, Protein: 44 g

Ingredients:
- 1 tablespoon extra-virgin olive oil, divided
- 1 stalk celery, chopped
- ½–1 large mild red chili, deseeded, finely chopped
- 1 ½ cups low salt vegetable stock
- 2 small bay leaves
- a pinch cayenne pepper
- pepper to taste
- ½ onion, chopped
- 1 leek, chopped
- 6 ounces puy-style dark green lentils, rinsed, drained
- 2 small sprigs fresh thyme
- juice of ½ lemon
- 2 white fish filets (5 ounces each), skinless
- lemon wedges to serve

Directions:

1. Pour ½ tablespoon of oil into a skillet and let it heat over medium heat. When the oil is hot, add onion, celery, chili and leek and mix well. Cook for a couple of minutes.
2. Add lentils and stir.
3. Add stock, thyme and bay leaf and stir.
4. When it starts boiling, turn down the heat to low heat. Cook until lentils are tender. Once lentils are tender, if there is liquid remaining in the skillet, then drain off the excess liquid.
5. Set the oven to broiler mode and preheat the oven to medium-high heat.
6. Place fish in a broiler pan with the skin side facing up.
7. Add ½ tablespoon oil, cayenne pepper and lemon juice into a bowl and mix well. Brush this mixture over the fish.
8. Sprinkle salt and pepper over the fish
9. Place the broiler pan in the oven and broil for a few minutes, until the fish flakes readily when pierced with a fork.
10. To serve: Divide the lentils in two serving dishes. Place the fish on top and serve with lemon wedges.

Chapter 11: Meat Recipes

Choosing the right meat cut is needed to reduce your cholesterol levels. The recipes introduced in this chapter will leave you wanting more without compromising your health.

Thai-Style Ground Pork Stir Fry with Peanut Sauce

Serves: 2

Nutritional values per serving: ½ recipe
Calories: 621, Fat: 25.6 g, Cholesterol: 76.8 mg, Carbohydrates: 68.5 g, Fiber: 4.2 g, Protein: 30.8 g

Ingredients:
For peanut sauce:
- 1 tablespoon creamy peanut butter
- ½ teaspoon Sriracha sauce or more to taste
- ½ tablespoon rice wine vinegar or lemon juice or lime juice
- 1 ½ tablespoons soy sauce
- ½ tablespoon honey

For stir-fry:
- 2 cloves garlic
- 2.5 ounces white mushrooms
- ½ tablespoon minced ginger
- 2 green onions, thinly sliced

- ½ teaspoon olive oil
- ⅛ teaspoon salt
- 8 ounces lean ground pork
- 3 ounces spinach
- sesame seeds to garnish
- cooked brown rice to serve

Directions:

1. To make peanut sauce: Add peanut butter, Sriracha sauce, vinegar, soy sauce, and honey into a bowl and whisk well.
2. Pour oil into a pan and let it heat over medium-high heat. Add pork and stir. As you stir, break the meat into crumbles.
3. Stir in garlic, mushrooms, salt, and ginger. Cook until the meat is brown.
4. Stir in the spinach and cook until the spinach turns limp.
5. Serve stir-fry topped with peanut sauce and sesame seeds over hot brown rice.

Grilled Pineapple Pork and Vegetables

Serves: 3

Nutritional values per serving: ⅓ recipe
Calories: 399, Fat: 15.2 g, Cholesterol: 110 mg, Carbohydrates: 23 g, Fiber: 4.2 g, Protein: 42.9 g

Ingredients:
- ½ can (from 8 ounces can) unsweetened pineapple chunks, with its liquid
- 1 clove garlic, peeled, halved
- 1 teaspoon dried oregano
- salt to taste
- ½ pound fresh asparagus, trimmed
- ½ large red bell pepper
- 2 tablespoons olive oil, divided
- 1 teaspoon ground cumin
- pepper to taste
- 1 pound pork tenderloin, cut into ¾ inch slices
- 2 medium carrots, halved lengthwise
- ½ bunch green onions, trimmed

Directions:

1. Add pineapple, garlic, oregano, about ⅛ teaspoon salt, about ¼ teaspoon pepper, cumin, and 1 tablespoon oil into a blender and blend until smooth.
2. Pour into a Ziploc bag. Add pork into the bag. After sealing the bag, turn it around a few times so that pork is well coated with the mixture.
3. Place the bag in the refrigerator for an hour.
4. Set up your grill and preheat it to medium heat. Grease the grill grate with some oil.
5. Take out the pork from the bag and place on the grill. The marinade is no longer required. Do not close the lid and grill for 3 to 4 minutes on each side or cook until the internal temperature of the meat shows 145°F on the meat thermometer.

6. Let the pork rest for 5 minutes.
7. Brush remaining oil over the vegetables (carrots, green onions, asparagus, and bell pepper). Sprinkle salt and pepper over the vegetables.
8. Place the vegetables in the grill basket and place it on the grill. Do not close the lid and cook for 6 to 8 minutes. Stir often and cook until tender.
9. Let the vegetables cool for 5 minutes. Cut the vegetables into bite size pieces.
10. Serve pork with vegetables.

Beef and Broccoli

Serves: 2

Nutritional values per serving: 1 ½ cups
Calories: 350, Fat: 12 g, Cholesterol: 104 mg, Carbohydrates: 20 g, Fiber: 3 g, Protein: 41 g

Ingredients:
- ½ tablespoon olive oil, divided
- 2 small cloves garlic, minced
- 2 green onions, thinly sliced
- 1 tablespoon arrowroot starch
- 3 tablespoons low-sodium soy sauce
- ½ teaspoon minced fresh ginger
- ¾ pound flank steak, cut into very thin slices across the grain
- ½ shallot, finely chopped
- 2 cups broccoli florets
- 6 tablespoons water
- 1 tablespoon coconut sugar
- crushed red pepper flakes to taste

Directions:

1. Pour oil into a skillet and let it heat over medium-high heat. When the oil is hot, add beef and cook until brown on both sides.
2. Remove the beef from the pan with a slotted spoon and place on a plate.
3. Add shallot, garlic, and green onion into the pan. Mix well. Stir often and cook for about a minute.
4. Stir in broccoli. Cook covered until tender.
5. Meanwhile, add arrowroot starch and water into a bowl and mix well.
6. Add soy sauce, ginger, coconut sugar, and red pepper flakes and mix well.
7. Add sauce mixture into the pan and stir constantly until thick.
8. Stir in the beef and cook for a couple of minutes.
9. Serve hot over brown rice.

Beef and Bean Sloppy Joes

Serves: 2

Nutritional values per serving: 1 sandwich
Calories: 411, Fat: 15 g, Cholesterol: 55.3 mg, Carbohydrates: 43.8 g, Fiber: 8.4 g, Protein: 25.8 g

Ingredients:
- ½ tablespoon extra-virgin olive oil, divided
- ½ cup unsalted, cooked or canned black beans, rinsed
- 1 teaspoon New Mexico chili powder
- ¼ teaspoon onion powder
- ½ cup unsalted tomato sauce
- ½ tablespoon Worcestershire sauce
- ½ teaspoon light brown sugar
- 6 ounces 90% lean ground beef
- ½ cup chopped onion
- ¼ teaspoon garlic powder
- cayenne pepper to taste
- 1 ½ tablespoons ketchup
- 1 teaspoon spicy brown mustard
- 2 whole-wheat burger buns, split, toasted

Directions:

1. Pour oil into a nonstick skillet and let it heat over medium-high heat. When the oil is hot, add beef and stir. As you stir, break the meat into smaller pieces.
2. Cook until light brown. Stir often.
3. Remove beef with a slotted spoon and place in a bowl. Do not discard the fat from the skillet.
4. Add the onion and beans into the skillet and cook until the onion is soft. Stir often.
5. Stir in spices and cook for a few seconds until you get a nice aroma.
6. Add tomato sauce, Worcestershire sauce, brown sugar, mustard, and ketchup and give it a good stir.
7. Add beef and mix well. Stir frequently until the beef is cooked and the mixture is thick.
8. Serve over buns.

Pan-Seared Steak with Crispy Herbs and Escarole

Serves: 2

Nutritional values per serving: 3 ounces meat with ½ cup escarole and ½ tablespoon herbs
Calories: 244, Fat: 11.8 g, Cholesterol: 59.2 mg, Carbohydrates: 10 g, Fiber: 8.2 g, Protein: 25.5 g

Ingredients:
- ½ pound sirloin steak (½ inch thick)
- ¼ teaspoon pepper, divided
- 2 cloves garlic, crushed
- 2 sprigs fresh sage
- ½ pound chopped escarole
- ¼ teaspoon salt, divided
- 1 tablespoon canola oil

- 2–3 sprigs fresh thyme
- 2 small sprigs fresh rosemary

Directions:

1. Sprinkle half the salt and pepper over the steak.
2. Place a cast-iron skillet over medium-high heat. When the pan is hot, place the steak in the skillet and cook until the underside is brown.
3. Flip sides. Add oil and garlic into the skillet. Place the herb sprigs in the skillet. Cook the meat until the internal temperature of the meat in the thickest part shows 125°F in the meat thermometer for medium-rare or cooked to your preference.
4. Take out the steak from the skillet and place on a plate. Place garlic and herb sprigs on the steak. Cover the steak with foil loosely.
5. Place escarole in the skillet. Add remaining salt and pepper and mix well. Cook for a couple of minutes until the escarole turns limp.
6. Cut the steak into thin slices. Serve steak slices with escarole and crisp herb sprigs.

Lean Lamb with Stuffed Zucchini

Serves: 2

Nutritional values per serving: 1 stuffed zucchini half
Calories: 511, Fat: 26.6 g, Cholesterol: 75.9 mg, Carbohydrates: 44.8 g, Fiber: 7 g, Protein: 26.2 g

Ingredients:
- 1 large zucchini, trimmed, halved lengthwise
- 1 tablespoon tomato paste
- ⅛ teaspoon ground cinnamon
- ¼ cup chopped onion
- 6 tablespoons basmati rice
- ¼ cup water
- 1 teaspoon salt
- ½ can (from a 28 ounces can) chopped tomatoes with its juice
- 6 tablespoons + 4 tablespoons water
- 1 ½ tablespoons olive oil, divided
- 1 tablespoon dried mint leaves
- ½ pound ground lean lamb

Directions:

1. Scoop out the seeds and little flesh from the zucchini halves. Leave ½ inch of flesh all around the peel area. So now you get zucchini shells or boats.
2. Add tomatoes, 6 tablespoons water, tomato paste, and cinnamon into a Dutch oven. Place the Dutch oven over medium heat. Stir often until the mixture thickens slightly. Turn down the heat to low heat and let it simmer until the stuffing is made.
3. Pour ½ tablespoon of oil into a small skillet and let it heat over medium heat. When the oil is hot, add onion and cook until soft. Turn off the heat and transfer the onion into a bowl.
4. Preheat the oven to 375°F.
5. Add rice, lamb, 4 tablespoons water, salt, and mint into the bowl of onions and stir until well combined.

6. Fill this mixture into the zucchini shells. Place the stuffed zucchini in the Dutch oven.
7. Turn off the heat. Close the lid and shift the pot into the oven. Set the timer for about 60 minutes or until the rice is cooked.
8. In case the sauce is runny, transfer the Dutch oven to the stovetop and cook until the sauce thickens.

Chapter 12: Desserts

Want to indulge your sweet tooth? Get creative with the different recipes you were introduced to in this chapter to satiate your sweet tooth and maintain cholesterol levels.

Chia Seed Wafer Cookies

Serves: 2 dozen

Nutritional values per serving: 1 cookie
Calories: 86, Fat: 4.5 g, Cholesterol: 10 mg, Carbohydrates: 10.5 g, Fiber: 1.4 g, Protein: 1.22 g

Ingredients:
- 1 ½ cups chia seeds, lightly toasted
- 2 egg whites
- 1 cup agave nectar
- 1 cup flour
- ½ teaspoon baking powder
- ½ cup non dairy butter, softened
- 1 cup coconut sugar
- 1 teaspoon vanilla extract
- ½ teaspoon salt

Directions:

1. Preheat the oven to 375°F. Line a baking sheet with parchment paper.
2. Add chia seeds, egg whites, agave nectar, flour, baking powder, non dairy butter, coconut sugar, vanilla, and salt, into a bowl and mix well.
3. Drop a tablespoonful of batter on the baking sheet. Leave about 1 ½ inches of gap between two cookies.
4. Place the baking sheet in the oven and set the timer for 6–8 minutes or until golden brown around the edges.
5. Remove the baking sheet from the oven and cool for 2 minutes. Remove the cookies from the parchment paper and place on a cooling rack.
6. Transfer into an airtight container. Store at room temperature. These cookies can last for about a week.

Nutella Banana Ice Cream

Serves: 5

Nutritional values per serving: ⅓ recipe
Calories: 281, Fat: 11.7 g, Cholesterol: 0 mg, Carbohydrates: 42.8 g, Fiber: 4.7 g, Protein: 3.1 g

Ingredients:
- 4 overripe bananas, peeled, sliced, frozen
- coconut sugar to taste (optional)
- ⅔ cup Nutella
- cacao nibs to garnish

Directions:

1. Add banana and Nutella into a blender and blend until smooth. Taste a bit of it and add coconut sugar or use any other sweetener if required. Blend until smooth.
2. Scoop into bowls right away for soft serve ice cream. If you want hard ice cream, transfer into a freezer safe container and freeze until firm.
3. Garnish with cacao nibs and serve right away.

Strawberry Lemonade Slush

Serves: 3

Nutritional values per serving: 1 glass
Calories: 60, Fat: 0 g, Cholesterol: 0 mg, Carbohydrates: 15 g, Fiber: 2 g, Protein: 1 g

Ingredients:
- 16 ounces fresh strawberries, chopped roughly
- 1 cup water
- ¾ cup lemon juice
- Stevia to taste
- 2 cups ice cubes

Directions:

1. Sprinkle Stevia over the strawberries. Toss well and set aside for 30 minutes.
2. Add strawberries, water, lemon juice, and ice cubes into a blender and blend until it gets slush like texture.
3. Pour into tall glasses and serve immediately.

Avocado Sorbet

Serves: 10

Nutritional values per serving: 1/10 recipe
Calories: 146, Fat: 0 g, Cholesterol: 0 mg, Carbohydrates: 8.2 g, Fiber: 5.8 g, Protein: 2 g

Ingredients:
- 4 cups unsweetened almond milk
- ½ cup Swerve or Stevia to taste
- 2 teaspoons mango extract or any other favorite extract of your choice
- 4 ripe avocados, peeled, pitted, chopped
- ¼ cup lime juice
- 1 teaspoon Celtic sea salt

Directions:

1. Add almond milk, sweetener, mango extract, avocadoes, lime juice, and salt into a blender and blend until you get smooth puree.
2. Follow the manufacturer's instructions and churn the sorbet.
3. Add the churned sorbet into a freezer safe container and freeze until use.
4. If you do not have an ice cream maker, pour the mixture into a freezer safe container and freeze. After about an hour of freezing, remove the container from the freezer and whisk well. Refreeze and beat again after 30–40 minutes.

Pineapple Sorbet

Serves: 18

Nutritional values per serving: 1/18 recipe
Calories: 62, Fat: 0.12 g, Cholesterol: 0 mg, Carbohydrates: 16.3 g, Fiber: 1.4 g, Protein: 0.6 g

Ingredients:
- 2 small ripe pineapples, peeled, cored, chopped into 2 inch pieces
- 2 ¼ cups sugar substitute or Stevia to taste
- 4 tablespoons fresh lemon juice
- mint sprigs to garnish

Directions:

1. Add pineapple, sugar substitute, and lemon juice into a blender and blend until very smooth.

2. Follow the manufacturer's instructions and churn the sorbet.
3. Add the churned sorbet into a freezer safe container and freeze until use.
4. If you do not have an ice cream maker, pour the mixture into a freezer safe container and freeze. After about an hour of freezing, remove the container from the freezer and whisk well. Refreeze and beat again after 30–40 minutes.
5. Scoop into bowls. Garnish with mint sprigs and serve.

Pink Grapefruit and Blueberry Popsicles

Serves: 5

Nutritional values per serving: 1 popsicle with sugar
Calories: 197, Fat: 0 g, Cholesterol: 0 mg, Carbohydrates: 43 g, Fiber: 1 g, Protein: 1 g

Ingredients:
- 1 ½ cups pink grapefruit juice
- Swerve or Stevia to taste
- 1 cup fresh or frozen blueberries

Directions:

1. Add all the ingredients into a blender and blend until smooth and sweetener is dissolved.
2. Pour into popsicle molds. Insert popsicle sticks in the molds. Freeze until firm.
3. To serve, first dip the molds for a few seconds in a bowl of hot water. It will loosen up. Remove and serve.

Berry Popsicle

Serves: 4

Nutritional values per serving: 1 popsicle
Calories: 238, Fat: 0 g, Cholesterol: 0 mg, Carbohydrates: 61 g, Fiber: 2 g, Protein: 1 g

Ingredients:
- 1 cup fresh or frozen cranberries
- 1 ½ cups cherry juice
- ¼ cup frozen orange juice concentrate, thawed
- ½ cup raspberries

Directions:

1. Divide the cranberries and raspberries among 8–10 popsicle molds
2. Combine cherry juice and orange juice concentrate in a bowl. Pour the mixture into the popsicle molds.
3. Insert popsicle sticks in the molds. Freeze until firm.
4. To serve, first dip the molds for a few seconds in a bowl of hot water. It will loosen up. Remove and serve.

Vanilla-Orange Freezer Pops

Serves: 5

Nutritional values per serving: 1 freezer pop
Calories: 53, Fat: 1 g, Cholesterol: 2 mg, Carbohydrates: 10 g, Fiber: 0 g, Protein: 2 g

Ingredients:
- ¾ cup orange juice, unsweetened
- Swerve or Stevia to taste
- ¾ cup low-fat vanilla yogurt
- ¼ teaspoon vanilla extract

Directions:

1. Mix together orange juice, sweetener, yogurt, and vanilla into a bowl. Pour into popsicle molds. Insert the popsicle sticks. Freeze until firm.
2. To serve, first dip the molds for a few seconds in a bowl of hot water. It will loosen up. Remove and serve.

Poppy Seed Fruit Salad

Serves: 2

Nutritional values per serving: ½ recipe
Calories: 178, Fat: 1 g, Cholesterol: 0 mg, Carbohydrates: 45 g, Fiber: 4 g, Protein: 2 g

Ingredients:
- ½ can (from a 20 ounces can) pineapple chunks, drained but retain the juice
- ½ kiwi, peeled, sliced
- ½ cup quartered strawberries
- ½ orange, peeled, separated into segments, chopped
- ½ cup seedless grapes
- ⅛ teaspoon grated lime zest
- ½ tablespoon honey
- 1 tablespoon lemon juice
- ½ teaspoon poppy seeds

Directions:

1. Place all the fruits in a bowl and toss well.
2. Add lime zest, honey, 2 tablespoons of retained pineapple juice, lime juice, and poppy seeds into a bowl and whisk well.
3. Pour the dressing over the salad. Toss well and serve.

Strawberries With Balsamic Vinegar

Serves: 3

Nutritional values per serving: ⅓ recipe
Calories: 60, Fat: 0 g, Cholesterol: 0 mg, Carbohydrates: 15 g, Fiber: 2 g, Protein: 1 g

Ingredients:
- 8 ounces fresh strawberries, halved or quartered depending on the size
- ⅛ cup white sugar or Swerve
- 1 tablespoon balsamic vinegar
- ⅛ teaspoon freshly ground black pepper or to taste

Directions:

1. Combine strawberries, sugar, and vinegar in a bowl. Keep the bowl covered on your countertop for 1–4 hours.
2. Sprinkle pepper on top and serve.

Strawberry Mousse

Serves: 12

Nutritional values per serving: 1/12 recipe
Calories: 94, Fat: 0.3 g, Cholesterol: 0 mg, Carbohydrates: 15.2 g, Fiber: 1.4 g, Protein: 8.2 g

Ingredients:
- ½ cup boiling water
- 6 egg whites
- 2 pounds 98% fat-free strawberry yogurt
- 6 teaspoons powdered gelatin
- 4 tablespoons caster sugar
- 1.1 pounds strawberries, hulled, halved

Directions:

1. Sprinkle gelatin over the boiling water. Keep whisking until gelatin dissolves completely. Let it cool for 10 minutes.
2. Meanwhile, add egg whites and sugar into a bowl and whip with an electric hand mixer until soft peaks are formed.
3. Put the yogurt into a mixing bowl. Add gelatin mixture and whisk until well incorporated.
4. Add egg white mixture and fold until just incorporated. Do not over-mix.
5. Cover the bowl and chill for 4–5 hours.
6. Serve mousse topped with strawberries.

Drunken Poached Pears with Hot Chocolate Sauce

Serves: 2

Nutritional values per serving: ½ recipe
Calories: 219, Fat: 0.9 g, Cholesterol: 0 mg, Carbohydrates: 49 g, Fiber: 7.2 g, Protein: 1.7 g

Ingredients:
- 2 Bosc pears, with stem, peeled
- 1 cup water
- 2 tablespoons cocoa powder, sifted
- ½ tablespoon honey
- 1 cup red wine
- ¼ cup caster sugar
- 2 inches strip orange rind

Directions:

1. Core the pears, only at the base. You can use a spoon or a melon baller to do so.
2. Add cocoa powder, sugar, water, and wine into a saucepan. Place the saucepan over medium heat. Stir until sugar has dissolved.
3. Stir in orange rind. When the mixture starts boiling, turn down the heat to medium-low heat and cook for about 25–30 minutes or until the pears are tender. Make sure they are not overcooked.
4. Remove pears with a slotted spoon and place in a bowl. Keep the bowl covered.
5. Add honey into the sauce mixture. Mix well and cook until slightly thick.
6. Drizzle the sauce all over the pears and serve.

Chapter 13: How to Cook Without Fats

Some form of fat or oil is commonly used for cooking. However, reducing the intake of unhealthy fats is needed to lower your cholesterol levels. A common assumption most have is that food cooked without any fat is bland because it brings to mind boring boiled foods. Well, this doesn't have to be the case anymore. You can enjoy delicious and healthy foods without using any fats!

Even if some oils are marketed as healthy, they aren't truly healthy as natural fats present in fish and seeds and nuts. Oils by themselves are pure fats and they contain more calories per gram than any other food you can think of. Therefore, avoiding them altogether is an excellent idea, especially if you want to tackle high cholesterol levels. Also, you don't have to worry because the healthy fats your body requires can be easily obtained from dietary sources and the list of foods you were introduced to in the previous chapters. Focusing on that is sufficient.

Now, coming back to cooking without fats, the first thing you must do is change your mindset about it. If you believe you will be eating boring meals and foods devoid of flavors, change your mindset. Compromising on flavors for the sake of health is not needed anymore. Instead, you simply need to make a few changes about the ingredients used, the cooking technique involved, and the cookware used. While cooking without fats, opt for non-stick pots and pans or silicone and non-stick ovenware. This helps obtain the desired texture without any oil or fats. Similarly, the best cooking methods for fat-free meals are sauteing, stir-frying, baking, grilling, roasting, and air frying. By making these few changes, you can dig into tasty meals without worrying about your cholesterol levels.

Cooking delicious and nutritious food is possible even if you don't use any fats. Use the different recipes introduced in this chapter to lower your cholesterol levels.

Broccoli Soup

Serves: 5

Nutritional values per serving: ⅕ recipe
Calories: 53.3, Fat: 0.9 g, Cholesterol: 1 mg, Carbohydrates: 9.8 g, Fiber: 2.9 g, Protein: 3.2 g

Ingredients:
- 12 ounces broccoli, chopped
- ½ cup finely chopped onions
- 4 cups fat-free chicken broth
- 1 teaspoon dried thyme
- pepper to taste
- low-fat cheddar cheese to garnish
- salt to taste
- 4–5 ounces baby carrots, finely chopped
- ½ cup finely chopped celery
- ½ cup fat-free half and half

Directions:

1. Combine vegetables, seasonings, and broth in a soup pot. Place the pot over high heat.
2. When the mixture starts boiling, turn down the heat to low heat and simmer until the vegetables are nearly cooked.
3. Add broccoli and cook until broccoli turns bright green in color.
4. Blend half the soup with an immersion blender until smooth.
5. Stir in half and half and heat well. Turn off the heat.
6. Ladle into soup bowls and serve garnished with cheddar cheese.

Vegetable Soup

Serves: 6

Nutritional values per serving: ⅙ recipe
Calories: 68, Fat: 0 g, Cholesterol: 0 mg, Carbohydrates: 15 g, Fiber: 3 g, Protein: 3 g

Ingredients:
- 1 onion, chopped
- 1 potato, peeled, cubed
- 1 large carrot, sliced
- 1 green bell pepper, diced
- 1 ½ cups finely shredded cabbage
- 1 cup cauliflower florets
- 1 stalk celery, chopped
- ½ tablespoon chicken bouillon powder
- ½ can (from 28 ounces can) whole peeled tomatoes with its liquid, crushed
- ⅛ teaspoon pepper
- 1 ½ teaspoons dried dill
- ½ teaspoon salt or to taste
- 7 cups water
- 1 teaspoon curry powder

94

Directions:

1. Combine onion, potatoes, carrots, tomatoes, bell pepper, water, curry powder, chicken bouillon powder, and pepper in a soup pot.
2. Place the pot over medium heat and cook until the vegetables are tender.
3. Stir in celery, cabbage, dill, and cauliflower. Cook until the vegetables are soft.
4. Blend the soup if desired. If you find the soup very thick, dilute it with some water.
5. Ladle into soup bowls and serve.

Black Bean Quinoa Bowl

Nutritional values per serving: 1 bowl
Calories: 500, Fat: 16.2 g, Cholesterol: 0 mg, Carbohydrates: 73.6 g, Fiber: 19.6 g, Protein: 20.4 g

Ingredients:
- 1 ½ cups canned or cooked black beans, rinsed
- 8 tablespoons hummus
- ½ medium avocado, peeled, pitted, diced
- ¼ cup chopped fresh cilantro
- 1 ⅓ cups cooked quinoa
- 2 tablespoons lime juice
- 6 tablespoons Pico de Gallo

Directions:

1. Cook the quinoa following the directions given on the package of quinoa. Measure out 1 ⅓ cups of quinoa and add into a bowl. Also add beans.
2. Combine hummus, lime juice and 1–2 tablespoons of water in a bowl and pour over the quinoa mixture.
3. Mix well and divide into two serving bowls. Scatter avocado on top. Drizzle Pico de Gallo and cilantro on top and serve.

Asian Noodle Stir-Fry

Serves: 2

Nutritional values per serving: ½ recipe
Calories: 279, Fat: 3.92 g, Cholesterol: 307 mg, Carbohydrates: 30 g, Fiber: 4.9 g, Protein: 30.4 g

Ingredients:
- ½ package (from a 9 ounces package) refrigerated angel hair pasta
- 3.5 ounces snow peas
- 5 ounces carrots, julienne cut
- 1 cup cooked, cubed chicken
- ⅓ cup stir-fry sauce
- ½ can (from 11 ounces can) mandarin oranges with its liquid
- 1 green onion, thinly sliced

Directions:

1. Follow the directions given on the package of pasta and cook the pasta in a Dutch oven or heavy saucepan. Make sure to add the snow peas and carrots while adding the pasta into the pot.
2. Drain the mixture and add it back into the pot. Stir in oranges, stir-fry sauce, and chicken.
3. Heat well. Garnish with green onions and serve.

Skillet Goulash

Serves: 2

Nutritional values per serving: ½ recipe
Calories: 365, Fat: 23.8 g, Cholesterol: 85.1 mg, Carbohydrates: 13.3 g, Fiber: 1.1 g, Protein: 22.4 g

Ingredients:
- ½ cup whole-wheat macaroni
- ⅛ cup finely chopped onion
- ½ can (from a 14.5 ounces can) petite diced tomatoes with green chilies, with its liquid
- ½ pound ground lean beef
- ⅛ cup finely chopped bell pepper
- 2 tablespoons salsa (optional)

Directions:

1. Follow the directions given on the package of pasta and cook the pasta.
2. Add beef into a skillet and place it over medium heat. Cook until the meat is light brown. As you stir, break the meat into crumbles. Drain off excess fat.
3. Stir in bell pepper and onion and cook until the vegetables are tender.
4. Stir in the tomatoes with its liquid and salsa.
5. Let it heat for a couple of minutes.
6. Stir in the macaroni. Heat thoroughly and serve.

Japanese-Style Ground Pork Stir-Fry

Serves: 2

Nutritional values per serving: ½ recipe
Calories: 373, Fat: 9.4 g, Cholesterol: 44 mg, Carbohydrates: 50.4 g, Fiber: 5 g, Protein: 23.5 g

Ingredients:
- ½ cup uncooked brown rice
- ¾ cup sliced mushrooms
- 1 ½ tablespoons grated ginger
- 1 small onion, diced
- 2 cups chopped leafy greens of your choice
- ¾ teaspoon rice wine vinegar or apple cider vinegar
- ⅓–½ pound lean ground pork
- ½ cup julienned cut carrots

- 1 clove garlic, minced
- 1 ½ tablespoons soy sauce, divided
- red pepper flakes or cayenne pepper to taste
- salt to taste
- sesame seeds to garnish
- thinly sliced green onion to garnish

Directions:

1. Cook the rice following the directions given on the package.
2. Let the cooked rice rest (covered) for 10 minutes.
3. Place meat in a pan and keep it over high heat. Cook until the underside is dark brown. Do not stir the meat until it is dark brown.
4. Now turn the meat over and cook the other side until dark brown. Do not stir the meat.
5. Now add ½ tablespoon of soy sauce and mix well. As you mix, break the meat into crumbles.
6. Continue cooking until the meat is brown all over. Stir every now and then. Transfer the meat into a bowl using a slotted spoon. Discard most of the cooked fat.
7. Add onion and mushrooms into the pan. Cook until slightly tender.
8. Stir in carrots and cook until tender.
9. Stir in garlic, ginger, vinegar, leafy greens and 1 tablespoon soy sauce. Cook for a few minutes until the greens turn limp.
10. Taste the mixture and add the remaining soy sauce if required.
11. Serve hot over hot brown rice.

Beef Taco

Serves: 2

Nutritional values per serving: 2 tacos
Calories: 579, Fat: 30.38 g, Cholesterol: 127 mg, Carbohydrates: 26 g, Fiber: 2.7 g, Protein: 48.3 g

Ingredients:
- ½ pound ground lean beef
- ¼ cup water
- low-fat cheese, shredded, as required
- 1 cup shredded lettuce leaves
- 1 tablespoon taco seasoning
- taco shells, as required
- pico de gallo, as required

Directions:

1. Add beef into a skillet and let it cook over medium heat, until brown. As you stir, break the meat into smaller pieces. Discard extra fat from the pan.
2. Add taco seasoning and water and mix well. Cook until thick.
3. Warm up the taco shells following the directions given on the package.
4. Fill the taco shells with the meat mixture. Place cheese, lettuce, and Pico de Gallo in each taco shell and serve.

Mango Salsa Pizza

Serves: 2

Nutritional values per serving: ½ pizza
Calories: 250, Fat: 4 g, Cholesterol: 0 mg, Carbohydrates: 45 g, Fiber: 8 g, Protein: 8 g

Ingredients:
- ½ cup chopped red or green bell pepper
- ¼ cup mango, peeled, deseeded, chopped
- ½ tablespoons lime juice
- 1 prepared whole-grain pizza dough enough to make a small 6 inches pizza
- ¼ cup minced onions
- ¼ cup pineapple tidbits
- ¼ cup chopped fresh cilantro

Directions:

1. Preheat the oven to 425°F.
2. Grease a round baking pan of about 6–7 inches with cooking spray.
3. Add bell pepper, mango, lime juice, onion, pineapple, and cilantro into a bowl and stir. Set aside until the pizza crust is ready.
4. Roll the dough into a round of 6 inches and press it into the prepared baking pans.
5. Place the baking pan in the oven and set the timer for 15 minutes.
6. Remove the crust from the oven. Spread the mango salsa over the crust.
7. Place the crust back in the oven and bake for 7–10 minutes.
8. Slice into wedges and serve.

Veggie and Hummus Sandwich

Serves: 2

Nutritional values per serving: 1 sandwich
Calories: 325, Fat: 14.3 g, Cholesterol: 0 mg, Carbohydrates: 39.7 g, Fiber: 12.1 g, Protein: 12.8 g

Ingredients:
- 4 slices whole-grain bread
- ½ avocado, peeled, pitted, mashed
- ½ medium red bell pepper, sliced
- ½ cup shredded carrot
- 1 cup mixed salad greens
- ½ cup sliced cucumber
- 6 tablespoons hummus

Directions:

1. Toast the bread slices if desired. These sandwiches taste better when you do not toast the bread slices.
2. Spread hummus on 2 of the bread slices. Divide the salad greens, cucumber, bell pepper, and carrot equally and place over these bread slices.

3. Spread avocado on remaining 2 bread slices. Close the sandwich by placing these slices over the stacked sandwich, with the avocado side facing down.
4. Cut into the desired shape and serve.

Chickpea and Chipotle Tostadas

Serves: 3

Nutritional values per serving: 2 tostadas
Calories: 347, Fat: 9 g, Cholesterol: 5 mg, Carbohydrates: 59 g, Fiber: 12 g, Protein: 12 g

Ingredients:
- 6 tablespoons fat-free sour cream
- ½ medium red bell pepper, chopped
- 1 clove garlic, minced
- 1 can (15 ounces) chickpeas, rinsed, drained
- ½ teaspoon ground cumin
- ¼ cup minced fresh cilantro
- 6 corn tortillas (6 inches each)
- 1 cup shredded iceberg lettuce
- ½ medium ripe avocado, peeled, cut into cubes
- ¼ cup salsa Verde
- ½ medium onion, chopped
- ½ cup vegetable broth
- 1 chipotle pepper in adobo sauce, minced
- ¼ teaspoon salt
- 1 tablespoon lime juice
- 2 plum tomatoes, chopped
- shredded reduced-fat cheddar cheese to garnish (optional)

Directions:

1. Set the oven to broil mode and preheat the oven.
2. To make sauce: Add sour cream and salsa into a bowl and mix well.
3. Place a skillet over medium heat. Spray the pan with cooking spray. Add onion and red bell pepper and cook until onion turns translucent.
4. Stir in the garlic and cook for about a minute. Add chickpeas, cumin, broth, chipotle chili, and salt and mix well. Turn down the heat to low heat and cover the pot. Cook for about 5 minutes.
5. Now take a potato masher and mash the contents of the skillet. Add lime juice and cilantro and mix well. If you are satisfied with the consistency, great, turn off the heat else cook until the desired consistency is reached. Stir often.
6. Place tortillas on a large baking sheet. Spray the top of the tortillas with some cooking spray. Flip sides and spray the other side as well. Place it in the oven and broil for 1 minute on each side.
7. To assemble: Distribute equally the chickpea mash, tomatoes, lettuce, and avocado among the tortillas. Spoon the salsa sauce on top. Top with cheese if using and serve.

Ground Beef and Potato Casserole

Serves: 4

Nutritional values per serving: ¼ recipe
Calories: 166.3, Fat: 4.1 g, Cholesterol: 32.5 mg, Carbohydrates: 18.5 g, Fiber: 2.9 g, Protein: 14 g

Ingredients:
- ½ pound 93% lean ground beef
- ½ can (from a 10.75 ounces can) cream of mushroom soup
- ⅛ teaspoon salt
- 2 medium potatoes, unpeeled, thinly sliced
- ½ cup chopped onion
- ⅛ cup water
- ⅛ teaspoon pepper or to taste

Directions:

1. Add beef into a skillet and place it over medium heat. Cook until the meat is light brown. As you stir, break the meat into crumbles.
2. Stir in onion and cook until the onion is tender. Drain off excess fat. Turn off the heat.
3. Preheat the oven to 350°F. Grease a small baking dish with some cooking spray.
4. Place half the potato slices on the bottom of the baking dish. Spread half the beef mixture over the potatoes.
5. Spread half the soup over the meat.
6. Repeat the potato, beef, and soup layers.
7. Cover the baking dish with foil and place it in the oven.
8. Set the timer for 40–60 minutes or until the potatoes are cooked through.

Chapter 14: 30-Day Meal Plan

Use the sample meal plan given in this chapter to focus on consciously reducing cholesterol levels! You can make any changes as per your tastes and preferences and use any recipe you fancy, as all recipes in the book are low cholesterol!

Day 1

Breakfast: Loaded quinoa breakfast bowl
Snack: Oatmeal energy bites
Lunch: Vegan "beef" stew
Dinner: Grilled pineapple, pork, and vegetables

Day 2

Breakfast: Chocolate almond bars
Snack: Tropical green smoothie
Lunch: Chipotle ranch chicken tacos
Dinner: Herby fish with wilted greens and mushrooms
Dessert: Strawberry mousse

Day 3

Breakfast: Mixed berry smoothie
Snack: Guacamole with sliced vegetables
Lunch: Avocado, tomato, and chicken sandwich
Dinner: Skillet goulash with easy rolls

Day 4

Breakfast: Overnight peach oatmeal
Snack: Papaya, blueberry, and avocado smoothie
Lunch: Rosemary garlic bean soup
Dinner: Black bean and corn rice skillet

Day 5

Breakfast: Cholesterol crusher smoothie
Snack: Stuffed mushrooms
Lunch: Middle Eastern chicken and chickpea stew
Dinner: Seasoned cod and Orzo with Parmesan and basil
Dessert: Vanilla-orange freezer pops

Day 6

Breakfast: Breakfast parfaits
Snack: Roasted chickpeas
Lunch: Cucumber and mung bean salad
Dinner: Mushroom bean bourguignon

Day 7

Breakfast: Avocado smoothie
Snack: Trail mix
Lunch: Chicken and white bean stew
Dinner: Ground beef and potato casserole

Day 8

Breakfast: Banana oatmeal pancakes
Snack: Nutty apples
Lunch: Vegetable soup
Dinner: Asian noodle stir-fry
Dessert: Berry popsicle

Day 9

Breakfast: Banana smoothie
Snack: Roasted chickpeas
Lunch: White bean and kale soup
Dinner: Tofu tacos

Day 10

Breakfast: Bulgur porridge
Snack: Spicy kale chips
Lunch: Veggie and hummus sandwich
Dinner: Fish with spicy green lentils
Dessert: Drunken poached pears with hot chocolate sauce

Day 11

Breakfast: Papaya, blueberry, and avocado smoothie
Snack: Edamame
Lunch: Chicken and apple kale wraps
Dinner: Barley, beans, and mushrooms with beans

Day 12

Breakfast: Mexican chickpea scramble
Snack: Apple and orange juice
Lunch: Lentil vegetable soup
Dinner: Eggs on beans

Day 13

Breakfast: Pineapple, mango and banana smoothie
Snack: Roasted chickpeas
Lunch: Creamy fettuccine with brussels sprouts and mushrooms
Dinner: Beef taco
Dessert: Pineapple sorbet

Day 14

Breakfast: Zucchini tomato frittata
Snack: Cucumber and apple smoothie
Lunch: Tomato soup with beans and greens
Dinner: Rosemary garlic ground lamb and potatoes

Day 15

Breakfast: Bulgur porridge
Snack: Tropical green smoothie
Lunch: Shrimp pad Thai
Dinner: Chicken sausage and broccoli rabe penne

Day 16

Breakfast: Fluffy egg white omelet
Snack: Cucumber and apple smoothie
Lunch: Mango salsa pizza
Dinner: Vegan lentil and mushroom shepherd's pie
Dessert: Chia seed wafer cookies

Day 17

Breakfast: Tofu scramble
Snack: Edamame
Lunch: Warm fish and quinoa salad
Dinner: Chickpea and chipotle tostadas

Day 18

Breakfast: Tomato and spinach egg white omelet
Snack: Banana smoothie
Lunch: Thai coconut fish curry and peanut rice
Dinner: Black bean quinoa bowl

Day 19

Breakfast: Breakfast parfaits
Snack: Trail mix
Lunch: Caribbean couscous salad
Dinner: Beef and bean sloppy Joes
Dessert: Strawberry lemonade slush

Day 20

Breakfast: Egg white muffins
Snack: Nutty apples
Lunch: Broccoli soup
Dinner: Japanese-style ground pork stir-fry with glazed ranch carrots

Day 21

Breakfast: Banana and blueberry smoothie
Snack: Stuffed mushrooms
Lunch: Quinoa salad
Dinner: Tuna noodle casserole with carrot salad

Day 22

Breakfast: Tropical green smoothie
Snack: Oatmeal energy bites
Lunch: Asian chicken lettuce wraps
Dinner: Lean Lamb with stuffed zucchini
Dessert: Pink grapefruit and blueberry popsicles

Day 23

Breakfast: Banana oatmeal pancakes
Snack: Guacamole with sliced vegetables
Lunch: Mediterranean couscous salad
Dinner: Kidney bean curry with garlic herb cauliflower rice

Day 24

Breakfast: Berry smoothie bowl
Snack: Roasted chickpeas
Lunch: Lemon garlic pasta with salmon
Dinner: Grilled chicken and sweet potato packets

Day 25

Breakfast: Fluffy egg white omelet
Snack: Banana and blueberry smoothie
Lunch: Veggie salad
Dinner: Kung Pao tofu with peanut rice
Dessert: Nutella banana ice cream

Day 26

Breakfast: Overnight peach oatmeal
Snack: Apple and orange juice
Lunch: Stuffed eggplant with couscous and almonds
Dinner: BBQ chicken tenders with roasted vegetable medley

Day 27

Breakfast: Tofu scramble
Snack: Tropical green smoothie
Lunch: Beetroot salad
Dinner: Rosemary garlic ground lamb and potatoes
Dessert: Avocado sorbet

Day 28

Breakfast: Tropical green smoothie
Snack: Stuffed mushrooms
Lunch: Chicken and broccoli quinoa
Dinner: Fish with spicy green lentils and garlic herb cauliflower rice

Day 29

Breakfast: Mexican chickpea scramble
Snack: Trail mix
Lunch: Black bean chili
Dinner: Creamy fettuccine with Brussels sprouts and mushrooms

Day 30

Breakfast: Berry smoothie bowl
Snack: Nutty apples
Lunch: Mediterranean three bean salad
Dinner: Pan-seared steak with crispy herbs and escarole
Dessert: Poppy seed fruit salad

Index

References

Cholesterol. (2018). National Library of Medicine. https://medlineplus.gov/cholesterol.html

Good and bad cholesterol: What's what and why does it matter? (2022, March 28). Cleveland Clinic. https://health.clevelandclinic.org/HDL-vs-LDL-cholesterol/

McDermott, A. (2017, January 23). *What's the difference between HDL and LDL cholesterol?* Healthline; Healthline Media. https://www.healthline.com/health/hdl-vs-ldl-cholesterol#hdl-vs-ldl

Seven foods to help lower your cholesterol. (2019, October 30). Heart Foundation NZ. https://www.heartfoundation.org.nz/about-us/news/blogs/7-foods-that-lower-your-cholesterol

Smith, J. (2020, March 26). *Eleven tips for eating out with high cholesterol.* Health Center. https://www.healthcentral.com/slideshow/tips-eating-out-high-cholesterol

Thorpe, M., & Lamoureux, K. (2021, November 23). *10 natural ways to lower your cholesterol levels.* Healthline. https://www.healthline.com/nutrition/how-to-lower-cholesterol#avoid-trans-fats

Tsao, C. W., Aday, A. W., Almarzooq, Z. I., Alonso, A., Beaton, A. Z., Bittencourt, M. S., Boehme, A. K., Buxton, A. E., Carson, A. P., Commodore-Mensah, Y., Elkind, M. S. V., Evenson, K. R., Eze-Nliam, C., Ferguson, J. F., Generoso, G., Ho, J. E., Kalani, R., Khan, S. S., Kissela, B. M., & Knutson, K. L. (2022). Heart disease and stroke statistics—2022 Update: A report from the American Heart Association. *Circulation, 145*(8). https://doi.org/10.1161/cir.0000000000001052

Printed in Great Britain
by Amazon

15964074R00066